Group economics lost in individualism

By: Patrice Shabazz

AF888721

For permission requests, contact:
Patrice Shabazz
Email: patriceshabazz39@gmail.com
Publisher: Exclusive Heights

ISBN: 978-1-969629-70-9
First Edition: 2025

Cover art by: Patrice Shabazz
Printed in the United States of America

Disclaimer / Introduction

This book is not socialism. Let's kill that lie up front. I don't believe in socialism, and I don't want anyone who reads this to twist my words like I do. Socialism says everybody gets the same slice no matter how much they worked, sweated, or sacrificed. That's not me. That's not us. That system kills ambition and makes the strong carry the weak.

I believe in accountability. I believe in ownership. And I believe if you work harder than me, you deserve more than me. Period. Nobody in this community I'm describing will be punished for hustling harder or rewarded for being lazy. We don't carry grown men. We don't water down work ethic. We build.

What I am laying out is group economics, not socialism. Group economics is simple: individually, we are broke, underpaid, and trapped in dead-end jobs. But when you add those wages together and move as one, you create leverage. You create ownership. You create options. That's the only way Black people bridge the wealth gap. Alone, your paycheck can barely pay rent. Together, our paychecks can buy the block, fund schools, launch businesses, and sustain generations.

This ain't about handouts. This is about pooling scraps to create feasts. Think Amish. Think Jewish communities. Think immigrant families that run bodegas, nail shops, corner stores, and farms. They don't wait on the government or outside investors. They recycle their own dollar. They keep their power close. That's not socialism. That's survival math and disciplined ownership.

In this vision, there are caps, dues, and entry fees. You put in to get out. Benefits are earned, not handed out. Everyone signs agreements, contributes labor, respects rules, and upholds standards. The work won't even feel like work because every hour you grind builds freedom for yourself, your family, and your people. The more we grow, the faster we flow. The more skills we add, the lighter the load becomes.

So let's be clear: this book is not asking you to pick up another man's slack. This book is teaching you how not to get trapped alone. It's showing you how to pool crumbs into bread, bread into wealth, and wealth into sovereignty. It's not socialism. It's not capitalism in its whitewashed, exploitative form either. It's cooperative survival — a blueprint for us, by us, with accountability and discipline at the center.

If you came here looking for utopia, you picked up the wrong book. If you came here ready to work, build, and multiply, then you'll see the vision clear: group economics is the only way forward.

Chapter 1: The Cost of Waiting

From the book: The Sovereign Blueprint

STORY: The Check That Never Cleared

It was always "next Friday."

For two years, Tyrone worked at a warehouse just off I-85. Hot summers, cold winters, his back breaking under quotas that kept rising while his hourly stayed the same. He was smart—real smart—but like most of us, caught in a loop he didn't design. Rent due on the 1st, water shutoff on the 10th, $4.89 for eggs and rising. The car needed brakes. His daughter needed glasses. And the landlord just raised the rent again "to match the market."

But Tyrone had a plan. Next tax season, he said, I'ma save $6k and move outta this apartment. Buy a little land maybe. Fix up a trailer. Grow some food. I'ma get my own, watch.

Next tax season came. His sister called crying—her baby daddy got locked up, and she needed help with daycare. He gave her $2k. Then his car died. Transmission gone. There went another $2k. The last $2k? He tried to "flip it" with a friend. They both got scammed.

Back to zero.

Another summer came. And still, he said: "I just need one more season. One more check. One more shot."

Then he caught a hernia at work. No insurance. Fired without warning. No savings. No lawyer. No land.

The check never cleared. The plan never started. The dream died in pieces.

PSYCHOLOGICAL BREAKDOWN: Why We Wait Too Long to Move

We've been taught to fear failure more than we fear stagnation.

The brain's trauma wiring favors survival patterns over liberation patterns. Meaning: it's easier to keep struggling inside a system we hate, than to build something new where failure means no net at all. That's why so many Black men stay "almost ready" forever.

We procrastinate with logic:

"Let me get my credit right first."

"I need more money saved before I move."

"My job's trash, but at least I got one."

"I'ma do it after my next raise/tax refund/income season."

But the deeper truth is fear of community risk. When you build alone, only you fail. When you try to organize 1,000 people and it goes wrong? That shame feels permanent.

White America has safety nets. Inherited homes. Parental help. Loans they don't have to pay back. Black folk? We got each other. And we scared to risk even that.

CORPORATE POV vs STREET POV

Situation	Corporate America	Street Reality
Job Loss	Offers severance, unemployment, COBRA insurance.	You just get fired. No check. No support.
Housing Crisis	Might sell a stock to cover the mortgage.	Late rent = eviction = shelter.
Retirement	401(k), pension, or family inheritance.	Work until your body gives out, then pray you can eat.
Health Emergency	Private insurance, sick leave.	ER visit = $7,000 bill or GoFundMe.
Childcare Costs	Employer-sponsored daycare.	$800/month or leave your child with whoever you can.

The system is set up to give them time… and give us trauma.

CENTRAL CONCERN: "But I Don't Have the Money to Start…"

This is the most common excuse we hear.

But money is not the first step. The first step is allegiance. Mental commitment. The decision to say:

"I won't wait to be ready. I'll prepare while I move."

The truth is, you will never "have enough" by their standards. If you wait to be approved by a bank, the system wins. If you wait to be debt-free first, inflation eats your buying power. If you wait until your personal life is perfect, you'll be buried before you ever get the land.

STRATEGIC SOLUTION: Build With the Broken. Move With the Movers.

Every Black community that succeeded did so with less than what we have now:

The Black Panthers fed thousands with food donations and volunteers.

The Deacons for Defense organized protection with old rifles and discipline.

The first Black-owned towns started with freedmen who had nothing but faith, skill, and each other.

We build with broken tools. Because we don't wait for permission.

The Sovereign Blueprint is built on phased development:

People bring what they can, not what they wish they had.

You start with 5–10 people. You secure land together.

Everyone commits a role: legal, plumbing, farming, vehicles, youth training, etc.

You don't wait until you're out of debt. You build so your children won't start in it.

"Don't raise your credit score. Raise your value score to the community."

You're not just moving out the hood. You're moving out of mental captivity.

FINAL LESSON: Nothing Worth Having Is Easy

Let me be clear:

You will lose people on the way.

You will be accused of cult-building, of being crazy, of dreaming too big.

You will cry some nights.

You will fight ego, jealousy, and your own doubt.

You will have setbacks.

You will see people walk away.

You may even fail the first time.

But if you don't start… you guarantee your failure before you even try.

"We're not building because it's easy. We're building because it's the only thing that can't be taken away again."

Waiting is the costliest thing you'll ever do.

Land moves.
Prices rise.
Systems tighten.
And your opportunity gets smaller every year.

Start with what you have.
Commit with who's willing.
Move in phases.
Plan in detail.

And build like your great-grandchildren already exist.

Chapter 2: We Had It All

STORY: The Fire They Couldn't Burn

In 1921, a Black boy was learning to fly a plane.

Let that sink in.

In a place called Greenwood—what the world now calls "Black Wall Street"—we had it all. Doctors. Hotels. Tailors. Movie theaters. Farms. Black-owned banks. Airplanes. Before integration, before EBT, before Section 8… there was ownership. There was pride. There was a street so rich in self-determination that white folks a mile over were jealous.

Then came the lie. A white girl screamed. A headline was printed. And by the time the sun rose, over 300 of us were dead. Over 1,000 homes turned to ash. The city sanctioned planes to drop bombs from the sky. Let me say that again:

They dropped bombs on Black families in America.

And we don't even teach that in school.

But Tulsa wasn't the only one. There was Mound Bayou, founded by freed slaves. There was Rosewood in Florida. Black Durham in NC. Boley in Oklahoma. Nicodemus in Kansas. Paradise Valley in Detroit. We had towns—entire towns—run, owned, and defended by us.

Until they were either:

Burned

Flooded

Bought out

Redlined

Or turned against each other

The fire wasn't just physical. It was psychological.

They didn't just burn our homes—they rewrote our memory.

PSYCHOLOGICAL BREAKDOWN: Erasure Is a Weapon

What happens to a people when they're told they never did anything worth remembering?

They become consumers instead of builders.

The system tells us:

"Y'all ain't never had nothin' unless we gave it to you."

"Y'all didn't build America—you picked cotton."

"Y'all too disorganized to run your own thing."

But the truth is: we've done it all before.

Psychologically, if they erase the proof, they erase the possibility. That's why most Black folks never even try to build community. We think it's never been done. We think we're the first to try.

We're not.

We're just the first to remember.

CORPORATE POV vs STREET POV

Situation	Corporate Memory	Black Community Memory
Legacy	Rockefeller, Carnegie, Ford, Vanderbilt—celebrated as builders.	Greenwood? Forgotten. Erased. Hidden.
Loss	Companies bounce back after a lawsuit or scandal.	One riot and a Black town disappears forever.
Ownership	White generational wealth builds over centuries.	We get a small win, and they burn it by morning.
Defense	White neighborhoods have police, guard dogs, security.	We defend ourselves, they call it a militia.

They make white legacy public history.
They make Black legacy conspiracy theory.

CENTRAL CONCERN: "If We Did It Before, Why Didn't It Last?"

This question comes up a lot.

"If we had Tulsa… why didn't it spread? Why didn't it survive?"

Here's the truth:

White violence. These towns were not failures. They were targeted.

Isolation. Most were standalone. No protection network.

No legal buffer. No land trusts. No nonprofit protections. No corporate shielding.

No scalable blueprint. We had culture—but not contracts.

Integration killed cooperation. After desegregation, we thought inclusion was the win. We gave up our bus lines, schools, farms, and barbershops to join theirs. We abandoned power for proximity.

So yes—we did it before. But we didn't protect it. We didn't document it. And now we're not taught it.

💡 STRATEGIC SOLUTION: This Time, It's Documented, Layered, and Protected

This book is the protection.

Now we move with:

Legal shields: LLCs, 501d, Co-ops, land trusts.

Security force: Legal, trained, de-escalation focused.

Cultural code: Written rituals, rites, and justice.

Scalability: This blueprint scales from 10 to 10,000.

Documentation: Contracts, agreements, handbooks, vetting rules.

Trade-focused education: No more degrees that don't pay. We build with skilled hands.

Most importantly: We build memory into structure.

We don't just build houses. We build oaths. Rituals. Monthly reflections. Symbolism. Elder councils. Story schools.

You won't just live here—you'll remember here.

And because we're decentralized—if one community is attacked, another rises. If one is infiltrated, another shields. If one falters, ten more hold the line.

We're not just rebuilding Black Wall Street.

We're building 1000 of them.

🗣 FINAL LESSON: They Took It Because It Worked

When white supremacy bombed Tulsa, it wasn't because we were "too poor."
It was because we were thriving without them.

It wasn't envy. It was fear.

Fear of a Black tax base.

Fear of armed, trained, spiritually grounded men.

Fear of self-healing.

Fear of financial independence.

Fear of a people who remember who they are.

They don’t fear our anger.
They fear our order.

That’s what this blueprint is: Black order.

And this time…

We move in silence.

We register everything.

We stay legally clean.

We protect our women and children.

We build across states.

We fund it ourselves.

We train our own lawyers, builders, doctors, and judges.

Because we had it all.

And now—we’re taking it all back.

Chapter 3 Modern Plantation: Rent, Debt & the Illusion of Ownership

Opening Story – The Lease With No Exit

Marcus had been living in the same apartment for six years. Every year, the rent went up. Every year, the carpet stayed stained, the plumbing got worse, and the neighborhood got louder. But he stayed—because moving costs money. Because breaking a lease costs money. Because a new landlord might deny him for having too many kids or not enough credit.

He thought about buying. His credit wasn't the best, but his cousin offered to co-sign. He started the paperwork—until the lender told him the monthly mortgage would be higher than his rent, plus insurance, plus property tax. Plus lawn care. Plus repairs.

So he stayed where he was. Paid more for less. Told himself it was temporary.

Six years became eight. He still called a landlord for permission to fix a leaky faucet. Still avoided the front office to dodge late fees. Still gave away 40% of his income for a space he didn't own and could be evicted from with thirty days' notice.

It was a plantation with Wi-Fi.

And it's not just him.

It's tens of millions of us—locked into cycles of payment with no equity. Leased lives. Rented futures.

Psychological Breakdown – Why Slavery Never Left the System

Slavery didn't disappear. It evolved.

The modern plantation doesn't need overseers. It has HR departments. It doesn't use chains. It uses credit scores. It doesn't whip you—it drowns you in bills.

Ownership feels like a dream because it's been structurally denied for generations. When your great-grandparents were denied GI Bills, your grandparents were redlined, your parents were preyed on with subprime mortgages, and you're told the only way out is $300,000 in debt for a home—you begin to normalize captivity.

You tell yourself renting is smart. That ownership is "too much work." That debt is necessary. That struggle is noble.

But the truth is, the system is designed to keep us locked in cycles of controlled mobility. You can move apartments, switch jobs, upgrade your car—but you're still paying into a system that owns you.

The plantation looks different. The power structure hasn't changed.

Corporate POV vs Street POV

In corporate America, rent is temporary. Wealthy people rent while they build or wait for the right investment.

On the street, rent is permanent. It's not a phase—it's a lifestyle.

In the corporate world:

You lease office space while your company scales.

You write off mortgage interest as a business expense.

You inherit property through family trusts.

In our world:

You pay rent until you die.

You hope your landlord doesn't sell the building.

You lose your apartment for a missed payment—and your kid gets uprooted mid-school year.

The same structure has different rules depending on your position in the system.

The Concern – "Ownership Just Isn't Realistic for Me"

Many people—quietly—believe ownership is a fantasy.
Too expensive. Too risky. Too complicated.
They've seen their family lose homes to foreclosure, or get trapped in loans they didn't understand.
They've watched neighbors lose houses in divorces, deaths, or market crashes.

So they settle.
They say, "I'd rather rent—it's safer."
They convince themselves they're being wise by avoiding ownership altogether.

But it's not wisdom. It's generational fatigue. It's trauma dressed up as strategy.

You can't escape the system by staying inside it.

The Solution – Shared Ownership, Not Solo Risk

You don't have to buy a house alone.
You don't have to own land the way they tell you to.
You don't need a 720 credit score and $20,000 saved.

You need community.

Here's the new model:

You and four others co-purchase five acres of land under a legal entity.

Each person commits labor instead of cash—or a mix of both.

Homes are modular. Utilities are shared. Infrastructure is co-managed.

Instead of a landlord, you have a contract.

Instead of rent, you pay into a group asset.

This is how wealth actually begins: not by waiting for approval, but by designing your own gate.

And in the full-scale model of The Sovereign Blueprint, it expands:

We buy 500 acres.

We divide by purpose: housing, agriculture, trade, spiritual use.

Members buy in through work, cash, or skill.

Nobody pays a bank. Nobody gets foreclosed.

Housing isn't just a place to sleep—it's a right of participation.

That's not a dream. That's a structure.

Closing Lesson – Renting is Not Safety. It's Disposability.

They told us renting was flexible.
They told us it was low-risk.
They told us it gave us options.

But the truth is, when you rent:

You have no say.

You have no power.

You have no equity.

You can be replaced in 30 days.

And when your entire people are renters—of land, of labor, of identity—you don't just lose your place.

You lose your legacy.

Ownership isn't just about a deed. It's about a root system.
And the longer you wait to plant, the more they pave over your opportunity.

You don't need to be rich to own.
You don't need to be perfect.

You just need to believe that freedom is worth the risk.

Because renting your life is the slowest way to lose it.

Chapter 4 We Are the Labor, We Are the Land

Opening Story – The Ones Who Built It All

Every morning at 5:15, Elijah punched in at the concrete plant.

He operated the forklift, loaded palettes, patched cracks, swept the gravel yard, trained the new hires, fixed the busted light above the loading dock—and somehow still got paid less than the guy in the office who didn't know how to restart the generator.

After three years, Elijah asked for a raise. His supervisor laughed and said, "You do great work, but you're not the kind of guy we promote."

He quit that night. The next day, they called begging him to come back—because no one else knew how to keep the place running.

Elijah realized something:

He was the business.

Not a part of it. Not a cog. He was the muscle, the memory, the machine.

And if he could build their dream…
He could build his own.

Psychological Breakdown – The Myth of Being "Just the Worker"

One of the most damaging lies we're taught is this:

"You're just labor. Someone else is the brain."

They divide us into roles:

"White collar" vs "blue collar"

"Manager" vs "worker"

"Visionary" vs "execution"

But in truth, the Black worker has always done both.

We've built every system in this country with our hands and our minds—then watched others take credit for the result. From farming to railroads to tech to childcare to culinary science, we have been the invisible architects.

But over time, that erasure becomes internal.

You stop seeing yourself as a builder.
You stop believing you can own anything.
You start saying things like:

"I don't want to lead, I just want to work."
"I'm not the business type."
"I don't know where to start."

But the reality is: you already started.
If you can work a job, you can build a system.
If you can show up for 40 hours a week for someone else's mission, you can learn to show up for your own.

You're not "just" the labor.

You are the blueprint.

Corporate POV vs Street POV

In the corporate world, labor is outsourced and undervalued.
On the block, labor is exploited and overhyped.

Corporate:

Pays you a wage.

Trains you just enough to keep you in place.

Protects the knowledge at the top.

Street:

Glorifies hustle but rarely protects the hustler.

Skills are passed down, but not documented.

Loyalty is expected, but not rewarded.

In both systems, labor is used—not honored.

Whether you're working at a warehouse or trapping out of a corner, your skills fuel the system—but someone else profits off the structure.

The rules are different. But the outcome is the same:
You build it. They own it.

The Concern – "I Don't Know How to Start Something on My Own"

It's one thing to know how to work.
It's another thing to know how to build a system that works.

That fear is real. A lot of us have skills—but we've only ever seen those skills used in someone else's machine.

So we believe:

"I'm good with my hands, but I don't know business."

"I know how to cut hair, but I don't know how to scale it."

"I can cook, but I can't run a kitchen."

But the truth is, they didn't build anything alone either.

Behind every corporation is a team. A structure. A process. A plan.
You don't need to know everything. You just need to plug your skill into a community that's building together.

In The Sovereign Blueprint, no one builds alone.
You bring your skill. Someone else brings theirs.
And together, it becomes a system.

The Solution – Structured Cooperation Over Isolated Hustle

The fix is not "go be an entrepreneur."

The fix is cooperative power.

Here's what it looks like:

A plumber, an electrician, a carpenter, and a roofer form a home restoration co-op.

They offer services to the community at low cost.

The community feeds them, supports them, protects them, and keeps their trade alive.

No middleman. No client chasing. No chasing social media likes for validation.

Same with mechanics. Same with cooks. Same with IT.

In the Sovereign model:

Everyone has a role.

Everyone contributes labor or skill.

Everyone benefits from the system that labor builds.

You don't need to start your own business.
You need to join a community that values your work, protects your time, and shares the rewards.

Closing Lesson – You're Not the Help. You're the Foundation.

The economy doesn't exist without you.
The harvest doesn't grow without you.
The homes don't stand without you.
The school doesn't run. The kids don't eat. The doors don't open.

You are the labor.
But more than that—you are the land.

You're not separate from the soil. You are the seed, the root, the rain, and the harvest.

And if we stop handing our labor to systems that don't value us...
And start planting that labor in soil we own...
We will no longer be workers.

We will be builders of a nation.

Chapter 5 A New Culture or No Culture At All

Opening Story – The Day the Drum Fell Silent

In a small Southern town once known for its vibrant festivals and porch-front storytelling, there lived an elder named Baba Kareem.

He had a wooden box filled with old carvings, cloths from West Africa, and an ancient drum he never let anyone touch.

Every summer, kids would come to his porch for stories. He'd bang the drum once before starting. Then he'd speak wisdom that wrapped the past, present, and future in one thread.

One summer, the kids didn't come.
Phones buzzed. TikToks looped. AirPods blocked his voice.
Even his own grandson rolled his eyes when Baba Kareem tried to explain the meaning of the carvings.

So Baba Kareem packed up his box.

He placed the drum in the shed, locked it, and never opened it again.

Years later, when the culture was gone, and nobody could explain who they were or where they came from…

The people said:
"We lost it all."

But the truth was: we ignored it.

Culture doesn't die.
It gets neglected.
It gets replaced.
It gets sold back to you in costume form.

If we don't build a new culture—one rooted in truth, not trend—we will be a people with no identity.

And no people survives that.

Psychological Breakdown – The Death of Originality

Culture used to be passed through presence.

Now it's passed through pixels.

We don't gather around fires—we gather around algorithms.
We don't sing freedom songs—we stream soulless beats.
We don't ask our elders—we Google strangers.

We've replaced:

Rites of passage with gender reveals.

Eldership with influencers.

Ceremony with content.

The effect?
A generation that doesn't know what it's a part of.

Psychologically, when a people lose cultural grounding, they begin to:

Accept any identity handed to them.

Make decisions based on trend, not truth.

Seek validation from the oppressor.

Embrace chaos as freedom.

Without a new cultural system, we will keep mimicking the very forces that destroyed us—wearing oppression like it's a fashion line.

Corporate POV vs Street POV

Corporate Culture sells you manufactured identity:

"Diversity" posters with no power behind them.

Culture days with fake inclusion.

Policies pretending to be principles.

Street Culture, once rooted in survival and truth, has been hijacked:

Real codes replaced with clout games.

Wisdom replaced with flash.

Pain paraded for profit.

In both realms, culture has been commodified.
You don't shape it—they sell it to you.

You don't live it—you perform it.
You don't grow in it—you drown in it.

Both corporate and street cultures now revolve around performance instead of purpose.

The Concern – "What Culture Do We Even Have Left?"

Many people quietly ask:

What's ours anymore?

Our names were taken.
Our food modified.
Our music industrialized.
Our language fragmented.
Our families broken.
Our holidays are pagan.
Our rituals erased.
Our memories replaced.

So what's left?

And more importantly—what's worth preserving?

The concern isn't just cultural. It's existential.

Because without a cultural foundation:

We don't know how to raise our children.

We don't know what's sacred and what's not.

We don't know when we're being disrespected.

We don't know when we're betraying ourselves.

That confusion makes us easy to control.

And if we don't address it, we won't just lose culture—we'll lose the ability to even recognize it.

The Solution – Foundational Culture by Design

We must design a culture of truth, function, and resilience.

Not built on trend.
Not tied to capitalism.
Not dependent on algorithms.
But rooted in memory, discipline, and legacy.

In The Sovereign Blueprint, culture will be:

Written – a creed, a scripture, a code.

Lived – daily rituals, monthly gatherings, seasonal rites.

Transmitted – from elders to youth, through stories, not screens.

Protected – by a cultural council that reviews trends before they poison us.

Celebrated – with ceremonies we define, not holidays they profit from.

This is not about going back.
It's about remembering forward.

We take the wisdom of our ancestors, the truth of our present, and the survival demands of our future—and shape a culture that builds powerful people, not programmed consumers.

Closing Lesson – Culture Is a Weapon or a Wound

Culture is not neutral.

It either:

Sharpens your purpose,

Or dulls your spirit.

It either:

Elevates your people,

Or entertains your enemies.

It either:

Teaches your children,

Or confuses them beyond repair.

If we don't build a culture, we will borrow one.
And borrowed culture will never protect you.

Because no culture protects what it didn't birth.

So we must ask:

What will our culture teach?
What will it reward?
What will it reject?
What will it defend?

And if we cannot answer those questions, we will be a people with clothes, cars, music, money…

But no compass.

A new world is coming.
And in that world:

Either you have a culture…
Or you become someone else's resource.

Chapter 6

Housing Is Strategy, Not Shelter

Opening Story – The Motel Mirror

Jameel never unpacked.
Every place he stayed was temporary.
Sometimes it was his cousin's couch, other times it was a woman he barely liked. A few times, it was a motel room where the TV barely worked, and the roaches crawled across the remote like it was theirs.

He'd stare in the mirror and wonder,
"How did I end up like this?"

It wasn't that he didn't work. He worked every day.
But the job barely paid enough to eat and fill the tank, let alone secure a place.
Rent was always just out of reach. Deposits? Laughable. Credit checks? Game over.

One night, his girl kicked him out after an argument.
No savings. No backup. No key to anything.

He sat in his car, cold, heart racing, and said to himself,
"This ain't just about shelter. It's about control."

That night, something snapped.
He realized what we all eventually realize when survival meets strategy:

If they control where you sleep,
they control how you live.

Psychological Breakdown – Housing Is the Battlefield

Housing is marketed as a personal milestone—
"Get your dream home," they say.
But for the working class and the poor, housing is a trap disguised as a goal.

Psychologically, lack of housing control creates:

Anxiety: You never feel settled. That mental instability leaks into every decision.

Powerlessness: You depend on the landlord, the job, the system. You can't move freely.

Desperation: You'll tolerate disrespect, abuse, overwork, or underpayment to keep a roof.

It becomes hard to dream past tomorrow when you're scared about where you'll sleep tonight.

But it goes deeper.
Lack of ownership creates a plantation mindset:
You wake up in their house, eat their food, work their job, and die on their terms.

Corporate POV vs Street POV

Corporate America pushes the fantasy:

30-year mortgages

HOA fees

$450K homes you'll die paying off

But what it’s really selling is a leash.

You become trapped in debt, tied to one location, and financially paralyzed. If you miss a few payments, they take back everything—and your "dream" becomes a foreclosure.

The Street takes the opposite approach—live light, keep moving:

Couch hopping

Short-term rentals

Hotel living

Section 8 if you’re lucky

But that version keeps you in perpetual instability.

In both systems, you’re either:

Owned by your house

Or you don’t own anything at all.

There’s almost no middle ground.

That’s where The Sovereign Blueprint steps in.

The Concern – Where Do We Live While We Build?

Most people don’t start with land or big checks.

So the real concern becomes:

"How do we house 1,000 people affordably while keeping flexibility, dignity, and ownership?"

We can't wait until we're rich.
We need transitional, strategic, scalable housing now.

And it must:

Be modular

Be debt-resistant

Be family and single-person friendly

Withstand weather

And allow internal upgrades

Too many Black men and women have died waiting on Section 8 lists or stuck in overpriced apartments with mold, noise complaints, and neighbors who don't care if your child sleeps well.

Housing shouldn't be punishment for being poor.

The Solution – A Tiered Housing Strategy for Freedom

Here's what a forward-thinking, sovereign housing plan looks like:

Tier 1 – Single Units (Low Cost, Fast Setup)

RVs (2020–2023 models, solar-ready, 5th wheels for families)

Tiny Homes (mobile and pre-wired)

Portable Cabins for singles and transitional housing

Tier 2 – Community Units (Mid-Tier)

Double-wides and triple-wides (energy efficient, built to HUD spec)

Duplexes / Quadplexes (great for multi-family or elder housing)

Utility hookups underground for aesthetics and safety

Tier 3 – Long-Term Builds

Modular-built homes with community labor

Adobe and brick options depending on soil and region

Earthships and passive solar designs for off-grid capability

Amenities and Infrastructure Must Include:

Fiber optic lines (bulk trenching once)

Central bathhouses (for RV rows)

Solar carports + water filtration

Clinics within 15–30 minutes driving distance

On-site mechanic bay

Community tool shed

Community garden, mini greenhouse, and walking trails

Closing Lesson – You're Either Anchored or Adrift

Housing isn't just about walls.
It's about strategy.
It's about anchoring your people in a space that multiplies power, not just holds bodies.

The plantation taught us that homes could be weaponized.
Ghettos proved it.
Redlining legalized it.
And landlords still profit from it.

But when we design our own blueprint, we change the game:

Children grow up rooted, not restless.

Elders pass on knowledge, not rent stress.

Single men stay focused.

Women feel safe.

Wealth compounds instead of leaking.

We don't just need homes.
We need power centers.

Because if you don't own the floor beneath your feet…
You'll always be at risk of eviction—from your dream, your dignity, and your destiny.

Chapter 7

Freedom Must Be Guarded: Security, Safety & Self-Policing

Opening Story – The Sirens Never Came

It was after midnight when the gunshots rang out.

Three shots. Then silence.

In most neighborhoods, someone would call 911. An ambulance might arrive. Maybe even an officer would knock on doors and ask questions.

But in this part of town?
Nobody came.

Marquise peeked through the blinds, heart racing, but he knew better than to open the door.
He'd seen too many setups. Too many "accidents" that never made the news.

The next morning, there was blood in the street. No police tape. No cameras. Just a stain drying in the sun.

He looked at his son, barely 7, and thought:
"We're on our own."

That's when it hit him:
We don't have security. We have surveillance.
We don't have safety. We have statistics.

Psychological Breakdown – The Trauma of Unprotected Freedom

You can't truly build anything if you don't feel safe.

And in Black America, we've been conditioned to see two things as opposites:

Freedom

And security

But they were never meant to be at war.
The real war is between sovereignty and surveillance.

Our people live in neighborhoods policed by people who don't love them.
Schools with security guards, but no safety plans.
Communities with cameras on every corner, but no healing when blood spills.

The result?

Hypervigilance – You never fully rest.

Paranoia – You assume betrayal before trust.

Helplessness – You stop calling for help because no one ever comes.

It's not just physical danger. It's psychological collapse.
When a people feel unsafe for generations, they begin to self-destruct.

Corporate POV vs Street POV

Corporate America's Solution?
Security guards.

Private patrol.
Billion-dollar surveillance contracts.
More fences. More insurance.
A response after the crime.

But it’s reaction-based. It's profit-based. It’s not protection—it’s liability management.

The Street Response?
Guns under pillows.
Dope boys as neighborhood “guards.”
Unwritten rules and hood codes.
“Handle it yourself” justice.

That creates a cycle of internal warfare —
Where revenge replaces resolution, and fear becomes a way of life.

Both sides fail.
Why?

Because neither invests in community-rooted, relationship-based safety.

The Concern – How Do We Stay Safe Without Becoming Cops Ourselves?

Building a self-sustaining community brings risk.

Jealous outsiders.
Internal disagreements.
Petty theft.
Major betrayal.
And the worst: conflict escalating into violence.

If we don't prepare a security system, the system will infiltrate us.

But we also don't want to replicate the trauma of the state. We can't become the very cops and courts we're trying to escape.

So the question becomes:

How do we create safety without slavery?

How do we protect without oppressing?
And who watches the watchers?

The Solution – Self-Governed, Layered Security Built by Us, For Us

1. Security Is a System, Not a Squad

We need more than guards.
We need infrastructure:

Perimeter cameras and lights (solar-powered, community monitored)

Neighborhood watch rotations with clear shifts and no egos

Conflict mediation teams trained in de-escalation

A secure entry point with a gate system and resident ID scan (not facial recognition)

2. Establish a Council of Fire (Community Justice Board)

This body:

Handles disputes between members

Reviews all security incidents

Determines consequences and conflict resolution

Rotates members yearly to prevent corruption

Must include elders, women, and youth reps

No more "he said/she said" with no resolution.
No more calling police as a first option.

3. Self-Defense Training Is Required

Every adult:

Learns CPR and trauma response

Gets basic firearm safety (licensed, not paranoid)

Is trained in de-escalation

Understands when and when not to use force

4. Vet Every New Member Thoroughly

Full background check (not just legal, but social history)

Reference interviews from prior workplaces or community ties

Mandatory 90-day probation period before full integration

Skill-based contribution or payment to join

This keeps energy pure and intentions accountable.

Closing Lesson – True Safety Is Built, Not Bought

You can't buy safety.
You can't pray it into existence.
And you damn sure can't vote it into place.

Safety must be earned. Maintained. Guarded. Rebuilt daily.

Our people been too used to being the last to be saved.

But in The Sovereign Blueprint, we don't wait for help.

We become the help.
We teach safety as culture.
We install justice as software.
We protect with purpose, not paranoia.

Because a people who feel safe?
They can build.

They can love.
They can rest.
They can think long-term.
They stop surviving and start planning.

Without security, freedom is a fantasy.
With it, freedom becomes a fortress.

Chapter 8

Feeding the Future: Agriculture, Animal Breeds & Food Control

Opening Story – The Grocery Store Shutdown

It was only three days.

Three days of trucks not running.
Three days of empty shelves.
Three days of chaos in aisle five.

Ms. Lucille stood outside her local store with her grandbaby in her arms, shaking her head at the yellow tape.

"No food today. Come back next week," the clerk said.

But there was no next week for people who live check to check.
No next week for single moms with two jobs and no fridge space.
No next week for elders who remember when they used to grow their own.

Back then? A yard was a garden.
Now? It's just grass.

Psychological Breakdown – Dependency is a Death Sentence

Food is more than survival.
It's psychological leverage.

Whoever feeds you, owns you.

And most of us been sold into ownership through convenience.

We don't hunt. We don't farm.
We don't store seeds. We don't collect rainwater.

And worse?
We think the system won't ever break.

But the pandemic showed the truth:

Supply chains crumble overnight

Grocery stores have only 3–5 days of inventory

Food deserts are real — and targeted

This ain't paranoia.
This is preparation.

Because when they control your food, they control your behavior.
They can tell you where to go, what to take, what to accept — all for a box of dry cereal.

Corporate POV vs Street POV

Corporate America's Take?

Genetically modified seeds owned by billion-dollar companies

Patent control over what grows and how

Factory farms with no ethics

Land owned by the top 1%, subsidized by your tax dollars

They don't feed the world — they feed profit margins.

The Street Response?

Food pantries

Hustling EBT cards

Stockpiling canned goods during chaos

Urban gardens, if you lucky

But it's not organized.
Not protected.
Not scaled.

It's survival-based, not sovereignty-based.

The Concern – Can We Really Feed Ourselves?

When people hear "grow your own food," they think:

That's too much work

I don't have land

I don't know how

But ignorance don't cancel reality.
Somebody gotta feed the future.

If we want to build a 1,000-person community, we need real answers:

What land do we need?

What crops grow best in our region?

How do we protect from drought, pests, and contamination?

Who leads the farm systems?

How do we process, store, and distribute food?

You can't have a revolution with no refrigerator.

The Solution – A Closed-Loop Food System Built to Last

1. Start With the Soil – Test Before You Till

Use independent labs to test for:

pH level

Heavy metal contamination

Nutrient content

Amend the soil naturally: compost, wood ash, fish emulsions, etc.

Choose heirloom, non-GMO seeds for long-term harvests.

2. Crop Rotation & Greenhouses

Rotate by season: greens in spring, root vegetables in fall

Use hoop houses or greenhouses to extend growing season

Build vertical gardens for compact food production

Train teens and elders together — combine memory with energy

3. Best Animals for Small-Scale Sustainable Communities

Chickens (Rhode Island Reds) – eggs + pest control

Goats (Nubian) – milk, cheese, brush clearing

Sheep (Katahdin) – no shearing needed, meat + wool

Ducks (Pekin) – eggs + less aggressive than chickens

Rabbits (New Zealand Whites) – high yield meat source

Bees – pollination + honey = income + healing

Tilapia tanks – aquaponics integration

4. Internal Distribution System

Farm store or co-op for member access

Stored in root cellars, deep freezers, and smokehouses

Barter system to reduce reliance on outside food chains

Canning workshops and preservation classes quarterly

Build grain silos early — wheat, corn, oats hold community power

Bonus Strategy – Fiber Optics & Agriculture Tech Integration

Use drone surveillance to track pest infestations

Use solar-powered sensors to monitor soil hydration

Set up fiber optic internet to run agricultural dashboards

Teach coding to youth so they can monitor systems and prevent sabotage

This ain't just a farm. It's an empire of nutrition.

Closing Lesson – Land is God, and Seeds Are Memory

To feed your people is to love them.
To feed them without poison is to free them.

Our grandparents had gardens with no blueprint.
No degrees. No machines. Just willpower and wisdom.

We got both.
We got tech, we got land, and we got ancestors guiding our hands.

If we control our food, we control our health.
If we control our food, we control our wealth.
If we control our food, we control our future.

The empire we build won't have fast food.
It'll have forever food.

No recalls.
No supply chain lies.
Just legacy on a plate.

You want freedom?

You better plant it.

Chapter 9

Housing the Revolution: Smart Structures, Camps, & Community Layouts

Opening Story – The Tent City That Could've Been Saved

Under the bridge downtown, forty-five Black men lived in silence.
Not by choice.
But because talking meant remembering how the system left them for dead.

One of them, 61-year-old Willie "Bonez" Thompson, used to own a barbershop.
He lost it after COVID.
Slept in a tent made from tarp, duct tape, and pride.

When the city bulldozed the tent city in the name of "safety," they never offered housing.
Just fences. And silence.

But imagine if instead of a bulldozer, we brought blueprints.
Instead of eviction, we offered equity.
Instead of silence, we said:
"Come home. We built this for you."

Psychological Breakdown – Shelter Ain't Optional

Housing isn't a luxury.
It's the foundation of human dignity.

When you don't know where you sleep, you can't plan, can't build, can't grow.
You're trapped in survival mode, and survival mode turns the smartest people into shadows.

They say "go get a job," but forget:

No address = no job application

No shower = no interview

No fridge = no health

The housing crisis wasn't an accident — it's by design.
And if we want freedom, we gotta start laying foundations made from stone, not promises.

Corporate POV vs Street POV

Corporate America's Approach:

Redlining and gentrification to rob us of land

Skyrocketing rent with no ownership options

HOAs and zoning laws that keep us out

Credit checks that disqualify the very people who need help

Street Reality:

Renting for decades with nothing to show

Couch-hopping, shelters, weekly motels

RVs turned into homes with no hookups

Family packed into 1-bedroom traps

And now?
They turn homelessness into criminality.
You get a charge just for trying to survive.

The Concern – How Can We House 1,000 People Without Becoming a Project?

Everyone wants to build something — but what we building matters more than just building.

We're not building a housing project.
We're building a self-sustaining empire that houses:

Families

Single men and women

Elders

Formerly incarcerated people

Children in foster care

And we need to do it without debt, without government grants, and without letting outsiders creep in and flip it.

So how do we design a village that feels like freedom — not another trap?

The Solution – Multi-Tier Housing with Purpose & Protection

1. Structure Variety Based on Needs & Season of Life

RV Units / Tiny Homes / Converted Campers

Ideal for single men or women

Easy to relocate, low-cost entry

Community bathroom & kitchen access

Single-Wides / Double-Wides / Triple-Wides

Permanent or semi-permanent structures

Triple-wides for families (4+ bedrooms)

Built with energy-efficient insulation

Duplexes & Quadplexes

Multi-family living with private entries

Lower land usage, easier to heat/cool

Perfect for elder units or family splits

Custom-Built Homes (Concrete Slab or Pier & Beam)

Permanent homes for community leaders, veterans, or long-term members

Solar roofs, rainwater collection, compost systems

2. Strategic Layout

Cluster by Vibe and Utility

Youth, families, elders, singles, healing spaces — each has its own cluster

Reduce tension, respect rhythm of life

Nature buffers (trees, fences, gardens) between zones

Emergency Escape Routes & Firebreaks

Gravel or dirt lanes every 200–300 ft

Water barrels and hydrants spaced accordingly

Everyone trained in evacuation drills

3. Amenities That Add Dignity, Not Distraction

Shared laundry facilities

Walking trails, bike paths

Outdoor gyms, basketball and volleyball courts

Fire pits for group talks and spiritual ceremonies

Monthly community repair day: everyone helps patch and paint

4. Utilities & Tech Infrastructure

Fiber Optic Internet laid early before structures go up

Solar panels integrated into RV and house roofs

Water filtration tower with gravity-fed storage

Backup generators or solar batteries for blackouts

Greywater recycling for gardens and trees

Bonus Strategy – Retired Buses, Shipping Containers, and Prefab Kits

Retired School Buses can be gutted and converted into mini homes or portable barber shops, mobile libraries, or elder lounges

Shipping Containers insulated and modified into dorms or tool stations

Prefab Kits ordered in bulk — 2–5 person assembly, delivered in crates

All builds require:

Land grading

Cement or gravel pads

Septic or community waste system

Security Without Over-Policing – The Housing Layer

Cameras on corners (not bedrooms) with community-elected monitoring teams

Each housing unit must check-in visitors

Random monthly background refresh for any non-members staying over 2 weeks

Men trained in "Guardian Patrols" – no guns unless cleared, body cams optional

Disputes go to Council of Fire, not police — resolution tiers in place

Closing Lesson – Home is More Than Shelter. It's Strategy.

You can't build a kingdom out of tents.
You can't raise a future inside a trap.

Housing isn't about square footage — it's about mental stability, emotional healing, and physical recovery.

The world left us with no land, no deed, no key.
But we can write our own titles now.
Not just on paper — in concrete, drywall, and sacred fire pits.

Our homes will hold babies and barbershops.
Mothers and midwives.
Builders and believers.

And when outsiders come?
They won't see "affordable housing."
They'll see the blueprint of Black sovereignty — brick by brick.

Chapter 10

Health is Homeland: Clinics, Healing, & Internal Wellness Systems

Opening Story – The Emergency That Never Made It

It started as a stomach cramp.
Maria thought it was just stress.
She'd been working double shifts, barely sleeping, and her insurance had lapsed two months ago.

By the time her appendix burst, she was laid across a friend's floor—sweating, shaking, whispering to God.

They called 911.
The paramedics came.
But when they heard "no insurance," they slowed down.
Didn't rush.

Maria died two hours later.
Over a $17,000 procedure that would've taken 45 minutes in a free clinic—if one existed.

That's why our new world needs its own health system.
Not dependent.
Not optional.
Mandatory.

Psychological Breakdown – The Silent War on the Black Body

The most radical thing you can do today?
Be healthy and free.

Because sickness is currency in America.
The more we ache, the more they make.

Black people:

Die younger

Have higher infant mortality rates

Get diagnosed later

Receive less pain medication

Get ignored more often

And the system is designed that way.
From hospitals to food deserts to fake wellness apps.
Your body is their profit.

And when there's no healing station in your hood, you normalize suffering.
You pass pain to your kids.
You hand trauma like a family recipe.

So we flip the script:
Wellness is the new weapon.

Corporate POV vs Street POV

Corporate America's Healthcare Game:

Use complex terms to gatekeep knowledge (deductible, premium, co-pay, formulary)

Create monopolies that jack up prices for insulin, antibiotics, and even Tylenol

Build hospitals in rich areas, urgent cares in white suburbs, and put "urgent" bills in your mailbox

Pharmaceutical reps get bonuses when prescriptions go up—not when patients get better

Street-Level Reality:

ER is the family doctor

Cousin who "used to work at CVS" gives advice

Popping 3 Excedrin for a migraine and hoping for the best

Mixing black seed oil with ramen

Getting mental health advice from memes and prayer

We not dumb.
We're underfunded, over-exposed, and tired of begging for care.

The Concern – How Do We Create Our Own Medical System Without Getting Shut Down or Overwhelmed?

Here's the truth:
Every Black community needs a healing house, not just a hospital.

But if you build it like they do—with too much paperwork, cold staff, and no soul—people won't come.

We need:

Trust

Herbs and diagnostics

Midwives and med techs

Affordable, accessible, protected systems

A place where your life is worth more than your copay

So how do we do it legally, logically, and with long-term sustainability?

The Solution – Hybrid Wellness Infrastructure with Holistic Backbone

1. The Core: Internal Clinic Structure

Phase One: Wellness Cottage

Built inside a 3-bed trailer or converted cabin

Staffed by 2 certified nurse practitioners or traveling RNs

Equipped with basic diagnostics (blood pressure, glucose, temperature, stethoscopes)

Storehouse of herbs, tinctures, vitamins, immune boosters

Solar powered, generator backup

Phase Two: Expanded Modular Clinic

Add separate rooms for dental cleanings, chiropractic adjustment, prenatal checkups

Trained staff in trauma care and CPR

Connected to external virtual care (telehealth deals for emergencies)

2. Mental Health Unit (The Quiet Room)

Weekly "listening circles"

Peer support teams with elder guidance

Meditation and breathwork training

Crisis response protocol for breakdowns or manic episodes

Natural remedies: Ashwagandha, magnesium, 5-HTP, music therapy, cold water dips

3. Birth, Death, and Rituals

Midwives on-site with birthing pools and sacred rooms

Death Transition Room for dignified spiritual farewells

Trauma-informed doulas, grief coaches, and herbal companions

Sacred bath traditions for newborns, ancestral name ceremonies

4. Healing Garden & Apothecary

Grow:

Mullein for lungs

Dandelion root for detox

Peppermint for nausea

Chamomile for sleep

Plantain leaves for cuts and bites

Store herbs in labeled amber jars

Create tinctures, balms, teas, and oils

Sell extras at local farmers market to generate clinic revenue

Supplemental Systems for Support

Medical Van Partnership: For major emergencies, build relationships with nearest trauma centers

Mobile Dental Days: Retired dentist visits monthly, does extractions, fillings, checkups

Vet Tent for Animal Care: Basic checkups for dogs, goats, and cats — run by animal-loving teens and trained elders

Community CPR & First Aid Classes: Every adult required to attend at least 2 per year

Biohazard Safety Protocols: Every trash, needle, and wipe handled with respect and protection

Special Note on Confidentiality and Trust

In our system:

No judgment

No police reports unless violence involved

No immigration status questions

No questions asked if someone walks in with visible trauma — just care

And every healer swears an oath:
"First, restore dignity. Then, restore health."

Closing Lesson – Your Health is a Homeland. Build It.

You can't lead a revolution while your teeth are rotting.
You can't fight for land while your kidneys failing.
You can't protect your children if you're too mentally broken to sleep.

This chapter ain't about medicine.
It's about sovereignty.
If we can't take care of our own wounds, we'll always run back to the people who caused them.

So we:

Train our healers

Protect our practitioners

Grow our medicine

Honor every heartbeat

Because true revolution isn't loud.
Sometimes, it sounds like a healed cough.
A safe birth.

A quiet mind.
A child who doesn't need the ER again.

We are the medicine now.

Chapter 11

Feeding 1,000 Mouths: Farming, Animals, & Food Security Without Dependency

Opening Story – When the Grocery Truck Stopped Coming

In a small Georgia town, the shelves emptied in 72 hours. A snowstorm had knocked out power for miles, but that wasn't what scared folks.

It was the silence.
No trucks.
No shipments.
No answers.

Mama Trish stood in the canned goods aisle with a blank stare.
She'd raised six kids off food stamps, stretched meals like magic, and always trusted the system to restock.

But this time, the truck didn't come.

The store manager locked the doors.
Fights broke out.
Babies cried.
People panicked.

And that's when Mama Trish whispered to herself:

"We should've learned how to grow our own damn food."

Psychological Breakdown – Hunger as Control, Food as Freedom

They don't need chains when they control your stomach. Every time you swipe EBT or tap Apple Pay for a meal, you're gambling with a system built on instability.

The average Black family:

Doesn’t own farmland

Doesn’t know how to preserve meat or grow kale

Thinks “organic” means Whole Foods and high prices

Relies on grocery stores 7 days a week

But the moment diesel prices rise or a shipping delay hits, your entire dinner plan collapses.

And let’s be real:
The system wants you disconnected from land.
Because land brings roots.
And roots grow resistance.

Corporate POV vs Street POV

Corporate America’s Control Over Food:

Genetically modify seeds so farmers have to rebuy every season

Create global trade routes where local farmers can't compete

Use chemicals to make fruit bigger, cheaper, and less nutritious

Package poverty meals as luxury (see: oat milk, kale chips, "superfood" quinoa)

Street-Level Survival:

Corner store hot chips and canned sausage

Dollar menu dinner

Church food pantries and school lunch leftovers

Urban legends about what's really in McChicken meat

"Don't eat before payday" becomes a lifestyle

We not lazy.
We just haven't been taught how to feed ourselves without a barcode.

The Concern – How Do You Feed 1,000 People Without Burning Out or Going Broke?

It sounds impossible, right?
You're not a farmer.
You don't have 800 acres.
You don't even like dirt under your nails.

But here's what nobody tells you:

A strong food system starts with 12 people and a quarter acre.
Because it's not about farming everything—it's about farming what feeds the system.

We need layers.
We need roles.

We need strategy—not slavery.

And we need a plan that works whether trucks show up or not.

The Solution – The Layered Sovereign Food Chain

1. Animals That Feed the Community

Chickens (Rhode Island Reds / Buff Orpingtons):

Egg-laying machines

Dual-purpose (meat and eggs)

Eat bugs, scraps, and weeds

Goats (Nigerian Dwarf / Kiko):

Milk producers

Brush clearers

Small footprint, big value

Rabbits (New Zealand Whites):

Silent, quick to breed

Lean meat

Easily housed in hutches

Tilapia or Catfish Tanks:

Controlled aquaponic systems

Fish waste fertilizes crops

No need for lakes or rivers

Bees (Honey = Medicine + Income):

Pollinate all crops

Produce wax, honey, and even royal jelly

Sacred protectors of the land

2. Crops That Matter Most

Foundation Crops:

Collards, turnips, sweet potatoes, okra

Beans, kale, carrots, tomatoes

All can grow in raised beds or barrels

Medicinal Crops:

Dandelion (liver)

Garlic (antibiotic)

Basil (anti-inflammatory)

Moringa (nutrient bomb)

Profit Crops (to sell or trade):

Sunflowers (oil, seeds, soap)

Lavender (essential oils, stress relief)

Peppers (dry for seasoning, trade as currency)

3. Growing Systems by Tier

Tier 1: Vertical Grow Walls, Hydroponics, Microgreens

Tier 2: Barrel Gardens + Companion Planting Beds

Tier 3: Chicken Tractors + Mobile Rabbit Units

Tier 4: Full Acre Rotational Plots for Corn, Beans, and Squash

Tier 5: Greenhouses & Cold Frames for Winter Crops

4. Preservation & Storage Strategy

Solar Dehydrators: Dry fruit, veggies, herbs

Canning Units: Pressure canners on propane stoves

Root Cellars: Underground storage for potatoes, onions, carrots

Freeze-Dried Reserves: Long-term emergency prep

Fermentation Stations: Kimchi, pickles, vinegar for gut health and flavor

5. Youth + Elder Food Alliance

Youth: Trained in aquaponics, chicken handling, food safety

Elders: Teach seed saving, composting, ancestral techniques

Weekly food festivals where knowledge is passed and meals are shared

Culinary apprenticeships for youth to learn prepping, plating, and feeding masses

6. The ReinStone Food Pledge

Every member will be asked to:

Volunteer 4 hours a month on land, animals, or kitchens

Attend 2 seasonal food education days per year

Learn 1 preservation technique and 1 growing method

Pledge to never waste food—compost or repurpose all scraps

Closing Lesson – If You Can't Feed Yourself, You Can't Free Yourself

We've been sold a deadly myth:
That freedom is a feeling.
Nah.
Freedom is a full plate you don't owe anybody for.

When your people can eat, you reduce crime.
When your kids can harvest, they grow pride.
When your community cooks together, war becomes unlikely.

This ain't about being farmers.
It's about feeding our future.

No more starving while the dollar store sells roaches and expired cereal.

We flip the food chain now.

And every fruit tree we plant is a middle finger to the same system that wanted us hungry and docile.

We'll never wait for the truck again.

Chapter 12

Housing for the Long Haul: Trailers, Tiny Homes, and Shelter Strategy

Opening Story – Four Walls, No Foundation

Jarell was 31, sleeping on his aunt's couch.
He had a job, no criminal record, even a side hustle fixing phones — but no address.

Every application asked for pay stubs, credit scores, and rental history.
He had none of that.
Not because he was irresponsible — but because he never had a fair shot.

He finally scraped together $3,500 for a used RV off Facebook Marketplace.

It wasn't much.
But it had a door he could lock, a bed he could crash in, and a reason to hold his head up again.

Now imagine 1,000 people like Jarell.
All with different stories.
All with one need: a roof that don't own them.

Psychological Breakdown – Shelter is the Root of Stability

We don't just need homes.
We need ownership.

Because without it:

Your landlord is your warden

Your lease is a leash

Your location can be weaponized at any moment

Most folks think owning a home means debt for 30 years and stress 'til death.
But what if we flipped that?

What if we built the village first,
Then gave the people a way to buy in without begging banks?

Security starts with shelter.
And shelter ain't just real estate.
It's mental space to plan your next move.

Corporate POV vs Street POV

Corporate America's Game:

Price out homes then rent them back to you at 3x the cost

Turn every apartment into an "investment property"

Deny loans to those without perfect credit or W-2s

Gentrify then tax you out of your grandma's block

Street Reality:

Crashing on couches

Paying $1,000/month for a motel

Living 5 deep in a 2-bedroom

Moving every 6 months with no stability

We ain't homeless from laziness.
We're unhoused because we weren't invited to the table.

So we build our own.

The Concern – How Do You House a Thousand People Without Losing Sanity or Land?

It's one thing to say "we gon' build."
It's another thing to house different family sizes, income levels, and personalities — while still enforcing community discipline.

We need layers.
We need a blueprint that can grow with us, not collapse under us.

You can't put everyone in the same structure and expect peace.

We need:

A housing strategy based on age, family size, contribution, and transition needs

Flexibility for growth, but boundaries for leeching

Units that can be financed, upgraded, or paid in work-trade

It ain't about aesthetics.
It's about function, freedom, and flow.

The Solution – The ReinStone Housing Blueprint

1. Housing Tier System

Tier 1 – RV & Converted Van Units (Singles, Travelers, Transitions)

For single men or women without kids

Easy to park, move, and maintain

Ideal for newcomers who are working their way in

Units priced under $7,000–$12,000 for quick acquisition

Tier 2 – Single-Wide & Double-Wide Mobile Homes (Small Families, Elders)

2–3 bedrooms, energy-efficient upgrades

Fully skirted and leveled on cement pads or gravel bases

Solar roof add-ons encouraged

Cost-efficient long-term living: ~$30–50K

Tier 3 – Triple-Wides and Modulars (Large Families or Dual-Income Units)

4+ bedrooms with option to split for two families

Ideal for full buy-in members who want legacy housing

Built to last 30+ years with concrete blocking, raised foundations

Budget: $65–90K

Tier 4 – Built Homes and Quadplexes (Permanents + Income-Generating Units)

Brick or concrete poured housing

Attached ADUs (Accessory Dwelling Units) for in-laws or renters

Quadplexes house 4 families with separate entrances, community patios

Built in zones closest to schools, clinics, and resource centers

2. Amenities Per Cluster

Every housing zone (20–40 homes) gets:

1 Community Center Shed (solar powered, with washing machines + library)

1 Playground Area (with shade trees and seating)

1 Emergency Bunker or Tornado Safe Room

Rainwater Harvesting Station + filtration system

Fire extinguishers + hand tools stored publicly

3. Construction Team Training

To sustain housing, you need builders in-house:

Train youth + reformed ex-offenders in HVAC, plumbing, electric

Hire a licensed master contractor to train and sign off

All homes built must pass internal inspection committee + fire safety

Apprenticeship hours = rent credits or future land stake

4. Financial Flexibility – No Banks, No Predatory Debt

Members can pay down rent-to-own units in cash or skill trade

Early contributors get discounted land plots or first pick

Monthly land dues = property maintenance, community security, and emergency savings

Internal lending circle (community bank) for interest-free building loans (max 5-year terms)

5. Peace Strategy – Housing Boundaries and Behavioral Rules

No unauthorized guests beyond 3 days

No subleasing or outsider rentals

Every home must be inspected yearly for safety and cleanliness

Community medics or social liaisons assigned per 40 homes

Conflict resolution handled by House Elders + Council of Fire

We not just housing bodies.
We're protecting minds and building legacy.

Closing Lesson – Every Roof Must Be Earned, Not Gifted

We don't give handouts.
We give opportunity to rise.

Every home represents:

A lesson paid in sweat

A life off the street

A chapter in something bigger than one person

The ghettos never cared where you laid your head.
They just wanted your hope.

We bringing it back.
Brick by brick.
Trailer by trailer.
Van by van.

Because even a shack is sacred when it's yours.

Chapter 13

The Income Engine: How to Create Internal Jobs, Trades, and Revenue Loops

Opening Story – The Barber Who Fed the Block

Marlon wasn't flashy.
He had a pair of clippers, a stool, and a tarp.
But every Saturday, that man made more impact than politicians.

He cut fades, lined beards, dropped game, and sparked dreams.
Kids left feeling handsome.
Grown men left feeling seen.
And everybody dropped something in the jar—even if it was just $3 and a soda.

When he moved into the new community housing zone, the elders gave him a shed and a seat.
Now he runs 6 chairs, teaches teens how to cut, and pays his land dues on time.

He never left the hood.
He turned it into a blueprint.

Psychological Breakdown – We Don't Want Jobs. We Want Purpose with Power.

The reason most people hate work isn't laziness.
It's misalignment.

When you're cleaning toilets for $12/hour while a guy in a button-up gets paid to mismanage Zoom calls—

You start questioning reality.

The mind rejects slavery in all forms.
Even when it's dressed in direct deposit.

People want:

Income that feels earned, not extracted

Skills they can pass down, not pass over

Community roles that feed them mentally, not just barely pay rent

That's what we build.

Corporate POV vs Street POV

Corporate America's Strategy:

Outsource labor while claiming they "create jobs"

Use metrics and paperwork to gatekeep promotion

Reward obedience, not talent

Eliminate departments, then call it "efficiency"

Street POV:

We barter before we bill

We learn by doing, not by degree

We hustle because survival forced innovation

And most of our jobs came with danger or disrespect

The gap ain't talent.
It's ownership.

We don't need jobs.
We need internal engines.

The Concern – How Do You Feed a Thousand People Without a Boss?

Every community dies the moment people have to leave to earn.
If you gotta drive 45 minutes to a warehouse just to make ends meet,
Then the land ain't free — it's just far.

We need value circulation, not just housing.
Jobs that:

Match personality and skills

Serve the collective

Allow wealth to be shared, not hoarded

But how?

The Solution – The ReinStone Internal Economy Framework

1. Tiered Job Systems (Based on Skill, Contribution, and Age)

Youth (Ages 12–17)

Entry roles: food prep, maintenance, garden rotation

Earn community credits, mentorship badges, and apprenticeship points

Early exposure to 10+ trades

Adults (18–59)

Assigned roles based on skill surveys and self-nomination

Every adult is either a Builder, Healer, Teacher, Grower, Defender, or Operator

2 main rotations per year to prevent burnout and build adaptability

Elders (60+)

Council, mentoring, light tasks

Legacy instructors for moral stories, history, and spiritual training

Receive full resource support in exchange for knowledge

2. Essential Internal Businesses (The Backbone 25)

Every community must launch with 25 economic engines:

Food Systems

Farming & Livestock

Meal Prep / Community Kitchen

Canning, Dehydration, Herbal Medicine

Construction & Maintenance

Electrical, Plumbing, Carpentry

Welding & Metal Works

Home inspections + solar installs

Health & Wellness

Natural Medicine & Midwifery

Fitness Coaches & Recovery Experts

Dental Hygiene, Hair & Skin Care

Education & Media

School teachers + Curriculum developers

Film crews, photographers, podcasters

Publishing and printing (books, manuals, forms)

Trade & Services

Tailoring, shoe repair, auto mechanics

Event setup, catering, logistics

In-house barber, stylist, spa services

Each of these becomes:

A training ground

A business

A trade legacy that can be passed down

3. Community Revenue Loops

1. Sell Externally, Circulate Internally

Example: Farm produces 10,000 lbs of food.

60% goes to community kitchens

20% sold at local markets

20% converted into long-term stored goods (dehydrated, canned, or traded)

2. Shared Profits → Community Funds

All internal businesses contribute a % to:

Emergency pool

Equipment upgrades

Youth scholarships

Travel and training fund

3. Credits System

Members earn "Rein Credits" for hours worked

Can be used for:

Rent deductions

Marketplace bartering

Discounts on tools, services, and future land stake

4. Ownership Through Contribution

You don't need a million dollars to own land.
You need a thousand people with vision.

After 12–18 months of contribution, workers earn:

Housing upgrades (priority for modulars or quadplex units)

Stakes in community business revenue (profit-sharing)

Voting rights on major policy shifts

Closing Lesson – If It Doesn't Feed the Community, It's a Distraction

We've glorified independence too long.
You can't fix a broken system solo.
You can't raise 100 children without a village.
You can't outwork oppression with 3 jobs and no plan.

But you can:

Build the engine

Train the youth

Create roles instead of waiting for permission

That’s the income loop.
Not just getting money.
But keeping it, building from it, and never needing their system again.

Chapter 14

The Discipline Zone: Cleaning, Security, and Order Protocols

Opening Story – The Broom That Built Respect

Before the trailers were leveled, before the gardens grew, before the street lamps worked…
There was Mrs. Geneva.

She swept the dirt roads every morning at 6 a.m.
Didn't ask for pay.
Didn't need a reason.
She said,

"If we don't clean it, we'll never care about it."

When the first community meeting happened, she stood up and asked one question:

"Who here knows what day it is to clean behind the gym?"

Nobody answered.

So she made the schedule herself.
Printed it. Posted it.
She birthed the order we take for granted.

Psychological Breakdown – Order Brings Peace to the Traumatized Mind

Most of us grew up in chaos.
Sirens, shouting, surprise visits, and survival instincts.

When your nervous system never knows what's coming next,
Disorder becomes your normal.

But truth is:
Peace without structure is an illusion.

The traumatized mind may crave freedom,
But it thrives in discipline.
Clean spaces. Clear roles. Predictable safety.
That's not control. That's care.

Structure gives people room to breathe,
because they know what's expected—and what's protected.

Corporate POV vs Street POV

Corporate America's Strategy:

Outsource janitorial staff but demand sterile office conditions

Hire security firms with no ties to the community

Enforce strict dress codes, camera monitoring, and badge entry while claiming "employee trust"

Street POV:

Cleanliness is often neglected until inspection time

Security becomes a personal hustle (e.g., big cousin, uncle, or local legend watching the block)

Safety depends on reputation, not formal systems

The problem?
We've been forced to react to danger instead of design for peace.

Now we build it.

The Concern – What Happens When People Don't Respect Shared Space?

No matter how beautiful a space is,
If people don't respect the rules, it breaks down fast.

One person leaves trash.
Another skips their watch shift.
Soon, the property looks abandoned, and the vibe shifts to survival.

No system can survive without:

Cleanliness as pride

Security as teamwork

Discipline as protection, not punishment

So we create a new model.

The Solution – The 3-Zone Discipline Framework

1. Zone 1: Cleanliness as Culture

Daily Assignments

Each unit is assigned to a "Clean Zone" rotation: bathrooms, hallways, public gardens, gym, outdoor trash stations, etc.

Rotations last one week at a time.

Teen and adult joint crews to build mentorship.

Community-Wide "Restoration Days"

Every first Saturday is a half-day of work:

Deep clean stations

Painting, planting, repairs

Led by elders and zone leaders

Sanitation Scorecards

Color-coded visuals posted weekly by the gym and food area

Green = Passed

Yellow = Needs improvement

Red = Immediate correction

No shame, just visual accountability

Trade Bonus

Those who excel can join the Professional Clean Crew for hire outside the community (event cleanup, AirBnB turnover teams, etc.)

2. Zone 2: Security as Sovereignty

3-Layer Security System
1. Roving Patrols

Rotating residents serve on the “Eye Watch”

Night shifts and midday shifts, especially during supply deliveries or community events

Equipped with radios, dogs, cameras, and visible jackets

2. Elder Watchtower

Front-facing residents (elders or stay-at-home crew) monitor cameras and report suspicious behavior or broken protocol

Trained to de-escalate without force

Monthly safety meetings

3. Rapid Response Crew (RRC)

A select group trained in:

Self-defense

Basic martial arts

CPR/First Aid

Emergency extraction (fire, weather, break-ins)

Recruited from ex-military, trained fighters, and respected leaders

They DO NOT act as police. They are protectors, not punishers.

No Weapons Without Community Vote

Firearms must be registered in the system and approved by leadership

No walk-around carry without designated roles

Storage lockers for ammo and community long arms, only accessed under emergency protocol

3. Zone 3: Order as Shared Honor

Community Protocol Board

All expectations are posted at:

Entry gate

Inside gym

Community kitchen

Online portal for mobile reference

Violation Protocol (The Honor Triangle)

Correction

A community elder or assigned mentor speaks to the violator

Restorative conversation: “What happened, and what needs to change?”

Restoration

A task, shift, or contribution is assigned to repair the impact (clean-up duty, apology circles, or trade-based restoration)

Reflection

If violations continue, the individual must attend a Circle of Fire:

A 3-person council

Decision made on next steps: guidance, temporary removal, or higher-level hearing

No One is Exempt

Title doesn't protect you.

Popularity doesn't shield you.

We protect peace above ego.

Closing Lesson – Cleanliness, Safety, and Order Are Forms of Love

You want to know how serious a community is?

Look at their bathrooms.
Look at who stands outside at night.
Look at how they talk when disagreement shows up.

Discipline is not about power.
It's about honor.

You don’t clean because you’re poor.
You clean because you respect where you live.

You don’t stand watch because you’re bored.
You stand watch because you believe peace is earned.

And you don’t follow protocol out of fear.
You do it because we’ve seen what chaos costs.

Now we write a new future—clean, protected, structured.

Chapter 15

The Education Engine: Community Schools, Curriculum, and Cultural Memory

Opening Story – The Boy Who Couldn't Spell His Name

He was nine years old.
Lived three trailers down from the entrance gate.
Couldn't read.
Didn't know his birthday.
When asked to spell his name, he wrote his nickname.

We didn't shame him.
We surrounded him.

Mrs. Zora, the retired teacher from Wilmington,
sat with him on her porch every morning with a whiteboard.
"Today, we write it right. Tomorrow, we remember it proud."

By twelve, he was reading community newsletters out loud at family night like a griot.

No more silence.
No more state neglect.
We educate our own.

Psychological Breakdown – Cultural Amnesia is Engineered

Colonialism didn't just take land.
It took memory.
Language.

Names.
Confidence.
Purpose.

They didn't just rewrite history books.
They erased oral traditions,
weaponized grading systems,
and made "intelligence" a eurocentric performance.

So when we say education, we're not just talking about math.
We're talking about memory restoration.

Every child we teach is a walking archive of resilience.
And every elder we honor is a living textbook.

Corporate POV vs Street POV

Corporate Model of Education:

Standardized testing that measures obedience, not intelligence

Underfunded schools in Black communities, over-policed and under-inspired

Curriculums built to serve capitalism, not community

College debt as a setup, not a launch pad

Street Model of Learning:

Learn to survive, not thrive

Hustlers become financial analysts without spreadsheets

Kids memorize music lyrics and slang but never see their own stories in textbooks

Emotional intelligence taught in the streets—but never honored in schools

We built brilliance out of scraps.
Now we give that brilliance a system.

The Concern – If We Don't Control the Education, We'll Repeat the Erasure

Every year, our kids get further removed from who they are.

They're taught:

Slavery was our beginning

Africa is poor

Business means suits

Success means leaving your people behind

They never hear about:

Moors building aqueducts

Black Wall Street's real economics

Indigenous science and land mapping

How to start an LLC, repair a transmission, or grow tomatoes

That's not a gap.
That's a spiritual trap.

The Solution – The 4 Pillars of Our Sovereign Education System

1. Memory First Curriculum

We replace colonial curriculum with sovereign truth:

K–3: Naming Ceremonies, Oral Traditions, Basic Language and Respect

4–6: World History from Indigenous, African, and Asian perspectives

7–8: Real American History: before Columbus, colonization, Reconstruction, and resistance

9–12: Financial literacy, land ownership, law basics, community building, trade mastery

Language Requirements:

Every child learns a second language from one of their ancestral lines (e.g., Yoruba, Nahuatl, Arabic, Swahili, etc.)

Cultural Memory Assignments:

Family Tree Projects

Interviewing elders

Rewriting "textbook lies" from their own voice

2. Skill-Based Learning Tracks (Middle School and Up)

After basic reading, writing, and math, youth choose or rotate into skill clusters:

Agriculture & Food Sovereignty
Grow, harvest, store, and sell produce

Health & Healing Arts
Learn anatomy, plant medicine, basic emergency care

Trades & Tools
Carpentry, electrical, plumbing, auto mechanics

Media & Message
Podcasting, videography, editing, script writing

Legal & Sovereignty Studies
Know your rights, contracts, how to file LLCs, record deeds, court survival

Economics & Entrepreneurship
Budgeting, investing, vending, scaling, taxes

Kids graduate with portfolios—not just report cards.

3. Community Teaching Pool

We treat our community like a university:

Retired nurses teach health basics

Ex-mechanics host trade labs

Artists teach design, branding, and content

Elders teach memory, values, and traditional knowledge

Book authors lead reading circles and publishing workshops

No degree required to teach.
Only wisdom, proof, and the ability to reach.

We create a system where kids say,

“I wanna learn from Mr. Kwame. He fixed the whole irrigation system.”

That’s impact.

4. The Academy of Fire (Youth Rites)

Every child, at age 13, enters a sacred journey of transition:

Girls: Voice Ceremony (honoring truth, clarity, and womanhood)

Boys: Flame Walk (trials of responsibility, restraint, and protectorhood)

Orphans or those without lineage: Name Year (assigned tribe name, taught roots, gifted a community family)

Final test:
Each youth teaches something back to the community before graduating.
This builds confidence, clarity, and contribution.

Closing Lesson – If They Don’t Teach You, They Can Trap You

The system doesn’t just fail us.

It profits from our confusion.

It wants you to think your people were born in chains.
It wants you to believe wealth comes from approval.
It wants you to believe your voice only matters with a degree.

But knowledge is not what they hand you.
It's what you reclaim.

And in this community, we don't wait on their books.

We write our own.
Teach our own.
And raise the kind of children
who can rebuild a world—from memory.

Chapter 16

The Health Grid: Community Clinics, Detox Protocols, and Natural Medicine

Opening Story – The Sick Can't Be Sovereign

He was 33.
Used to be fast. Sharp. Could wire a house blindfolded.
Now? Always coughing.
He drank three sodas a day, smoked gas station cigars, and lived off corner-store food.
One day, he collapsed while fixing an irrigation pump.

We carried him to the community healing house.
Mama Kemi, the herbalist, didn't panic.
She placed roots in water, crushed black seeds, burned eucalyptus, and laid hands on his chest.
No hospital. No insurance. No ER wait times.
Three days later, he stood up.

That was the day we realized:
No clinic means no freedom.
No healing means no future.

Psychological Breakdown – They Taught Us to Be Addicted to Our Own Death

The food.
The stress.
The chemicals.
The sugar.
The silence about our pain.
It was never about convenience.
It was about control.

You can't lead if you're inflamed.
You can't build if your body is breaking.
You can't think straight if your gut is rotting.

They trained us to destroy ourselves slowly—
then shamed us for being too tired to fight back.

But health ain't a luxury.
It's a weapon of liberation.

Corporate POV vs Street POV

Corporate System (Medical Complex):

Prescribes pills, not prevention

Builds hospitals, but keeps prices hidden

Promotes fast food and then sells blood pressure meds

Ignores root causes—focuses on lifelong customers

Street Culture:

Distrusts doctors (for good reason)

Self-medicates with weed, liquor, or denial

Eats cheap to survive

Accepts sickness as "normal" because healing seems expensive or unreachable

But what if we removed the middleman?
What if we built healing into the land?

The Concern – If We Don't Control the Healing, We Inherit the Dying

Diseases are rising.
Not because of genetics.
But because of profit paths.

Black men dying from colon cancer by 40

Black women having hysterectomies they didn't need

Children developing asthma, eczema, and ADHD at alarming rates

Emotional trauma passed down, never detoxed

This isn't bad luck.
It's system design.

And if we don't create our own grid of health,
we'll keep burying brilliance before it blooms.

The Solution – The Community Health Grid Blueprint

1. The Healing House

Each community has a central wellness hub:

Herbal apothecary with fresh and dried medicinal plants

Detox rooms with sauna tents, hot/cold therapy, and breathwork sessions

Counseling circle led by trained mental health elders

Non-toxic childbirth room for natural births

Fasting supervision and gut reset protocols

Male and female health-specific workshops (fibroids, prostate, fertility)

Staff is a mix of:

Trained herbalists

Retired nurses and doulas

Bodyworkers (massage, acupuncture, reflexology)

Nutritionists and fitness mentors

No insurance. No prescriptions.
Just truth and care.

2. The Food = Medicine Program

We feed the village with intention:

Community kitchen cooks from scratch

Monthly "reset weeks" with detox broth, smoothies, and fasting breaks

Kids learn to prepare ancestral dishes—sorghum, greens, bone broth, fermented foods

Every food grown is labeled: healing, neutral, or harmful

The community learns:

"If I wouldn't feed it to an elder recovering,
I shouldn't feed it to myself every day."

3. The Monthly Cleanse Protocol

Every 30 days, the community resets:

Day 1–2: Juice or broth fast

Day 3–4: Raw foods only

Day 5–6: Cooked healing meals

Day 7: Colon support (flax, bentonite, herbal blends)

People track how they feel, what clears up, what comes out. And the kids participate with their own versions—fruit-only days or no-junk weeks.

This isn't a trend.
It's a discipline.

4. The Plant Pharmacy & Land Grown Medicine

On the land, we grow:

Mullein (lungs)

Dandelion (liver and blood)

Black seed (immunity)

Elderberry (cold/flu)

Ginger, turmeric, burdock, ashwagandha, red clover, hibiscus

Every home gets a starter herb box.
Every elder gets free tinctures and teas.
Every child learns:

"This leaf can save your life.
Know it. Grow it."

5. Sacred Silence Days & Mental Health Walks

We protect the mind as much as the body:

No phones for 24 hours each month

Group walks in silence through the land trails

Night talks under firelight led by community elders

Grief circles where people can cry without judgment

Journaling hours and meditation sessions

Mental health ain't soft.
It's survival.

We don't diagnose everyone.
We hold them.

Closing Lesson – A Sick Village Can't Fight, Heal, or Lead

America gave us poison—then blamed us for the symptoms.
It flooded our stores with sugar, our air with chemicals, our communities with fast death.

Then said:

“You need us to survive.”

But now we know—
health was stolen, not lost.

We take it back one fast, one herb, one healing circle at a time.

Because you can’t build sovereignty with broken guts,
toxic wombs, foggy minds, or numb spirits.

Healing is our revolution.
Health is our inheritance.
And this time—
nobody’s selling it back to us.

Chapter 17

The Internal Economy: Community Currency, Savings Pools, and Debt Resistance

Opening Story – The Bank of Us

We didn't start with much.
A few hundred dollars each.
Some gave cash. Some gave tools.
Some gave time.

We called it The Pot.

At first, it was just emergency money—
to fix a van, cover a medical scare, or help someone pay off probation fees.

But then it grew.

We wrote bylaws.
Assigned keepers.
Tracked interest-free loans.
And just like that…

We became our own bank.

No suits. No credit checks. No 19% APR.
Just trust, accountability, and a shared goal:

To never let the system eat one of us alive again.

Psychological Breakdown – They Taught Us to Beg for What We Already Built

We make the culture.
We power the labor force.
We spend more than any group per capita.
But when it's time for help,
we're told we're broke.

We're not broke.
We're broken up—isolated, divided, scattered.

They taught us to flex in front of each other,
but fold in front of the lender.

Why?

Because they knew:
a unified dollar is a dangerous dollar.
A sovereign dollar don't beg.
It builds.

Corporate POV vs Street POV

Corporate Banking System:

Charges you to access your own money

Gives pennies on savings, then lends your money at 20x profit

Denies you loans, but offers you overdraft fees

Targets Black folks with payday loans, subprime mortgages, and credit traps

Keeps wealth centralized and invisible

Street Response:

Hides cash in shoeboxes

Distrusts banks after generations of redlining

Gets caught in cycles of debt from street loans or high-interest traps

Doesn’t know how to build collective wealth—only individual hustle

But neither side builds safety.
The corporate side exploits.
The street side isolates.

We need a third way.
Ours.

The Concern – If We Don't Control Our Dollar, Our Dollar Controls Us

Look around.

$50 billion spent annually by Black consumers on hair care, fashion, and alcohol

Average Black family net worth: $24,000

Average white family: $188,000

Only 4% of Black-owned businesses have paid employees

Only 2% of community dollars circulate more than once

We’re making millions, but living like we don’t.

Because money without structure is just fuel for someone else's fire.

If we don't own our own financial lifeline,
we'll always be dancing on the edge of eviction, stress, and survival-mode thinking.

The Solution – The Internal Economy Blueprint

1. The Sovereign Pot: Emergency + Expansion Fund

Every member contributes:

$20–$200/month depending on income or service bartering

Tracked with open ledgers, receipts, and rotating trusted keepers

No penalties, but built-in reviews every 90 days

Every dollar logged and explained at town forums

Use cases:

Emergency vehicle repairs

Legal help (bail, lawyer retainers)

Business seed money

Equipment pool (shared cameras, tools, laptops)

This fund is our buffer against chaos.

2. The Monthly Debt Kill Missions

Each month, the community targets ONE person's financial burden:

Credit card debt

Student loans

Court fines

Payday loan traps

Car title loans

The goal:

Free one soldier, so they can help free the next.

It's a chain reaction of relief.

People post receipts, make financial plans, and go through an "accountability circle" before qualifying.

No shame.
No judgment.
Just forward.

3. Barter Economy + Service Credits

Not everyone has cash.
But everyone has value.

We set up a barter board:

A cook offers 3 meal preps in exchange for a haircut

A mechanic offers brake jobs for an oil change and 2 hours of farm help

A seamstress trades tailoring for babysitting time

No IRS. No taxes. No debt. Just skill for skill.

This builds dignity, not dependency.
And people gain worth through giving.

4. Community Business Shares

All community-run businesses:

Donate 5–10% of net income monthly into the Internal Economy

In return, get tax/legal protection, guaranteed customers, and pooled promotion

Businesses are:

Mechanic shop

Salon & braiding suite

Content studio

Food co-op

Teaching trades to kids (with pay)

As these grow, profits are:

Split into Roth IRAs, pension-style pools, and reinvestment

Partially gifted back to startup contributors annually

Matched with emergency fund for self-insurance

This creates the retirement plans we were never given.

5. The Credit Resistance Strategy

We teach members:

How to build business credit

How to use 0% APR cards only for strategic investments

How to exit predatory loan cycles

How to dispute unfair collections

How to build "buy now, pay never" systems: cash-only group purchases

We teach debt like it's warfare—because it is.

And we raise children with the mindset that if you can't buy two,
you shouldn't finance one.

Closing Lesson – A Dollar With No Mission is a Weapon Turned Backward

They convinced us we needed them to access our own power.
They turned our dollar into a leash.
They mocked us for being poor while making billions off our habits.

But now?
We build our own vault.
We flip the system inside out.
We create financial rituals, savings cultures, barter honor codes, and emergency sanctuaries.

Because one day of freedom costs more than a lifetime of comfort in chains.

And we'd rather pool our pennies in truth—
than chase their dollars in silence.

Chapter 18

Building Black Wealth That Lasts: Land Trusts, Group Ownership, and Multi-Generational Moves

Opening Story – The Dirt We Died For

Grandpa used to sit on the porch and say:

"You don't really own nothing till you own what your blood soaks into."

He bought 5 acres in '72.
Worked three jobs. Built a little home with his hands.
Planted a pecan tree every year a grandchild was born.
By the time he passed, there were 14 trees and a yard full of family.

Then the city came.

Zoning change.
Property taxes doubled.
Grandkids didn't want to farm.
The land sat still… until it sold for a fraction of its worth.

Now, there's a gated development sitting on top of his sweat.

He died owning it.
We lived long enough to lose it.

Psychological Breakdown – Why We Struggle to Think 3 Generations Ahead

They trained us to chase flash over foundation.
Taught us to value ownership of brands over land.

We celebrate car notes more than deeds.
We inherit stress, not property.
And even when we do get land, we don't protect it.

Why?

Because nobody taught us estate planning.
Nobody explained the probate game.
Nobody showed us how they legally rob your legacy with a smile.

And deep down, we fear permanence—
because we were never given security.

So we treat everything like it's temporary.

Corporate POV vs Street POV

Corporate Real Estate World:

Uses LLCs, trusts, and holding companies to protect wealth

Buys land in depressed Black neighborhoods and flips it with rezoning

Uses tax loopholes to pay $0 on multi-million-dollar portfolios

Pays architects and politicians to make gentrification look like "progress"

Buys silence by offering quick cash to grieving families with deeds

Street Response:

Rents forever and calls it “flexible”

Lives in homes with no wills, no titles, no protections

Believes property is “for rich folks”

Gets pushed out during every wave of gentrification

Buys into short-term hustles, not long-term holdings

The street never stood a chance against the blueprint they never gave us.

But now?
We write our own.

The Concern – If We Don’t Own Dirt, We’ll Be Buried in Debt on Someone Else’s Land

This is war.
The silent kind.

Where they buy your grandma’s house from your cousin for $30K,
then turn it into a $2,500/month Airbnb.

Where you think you’re free, but every paycheck goes to rent,
and every rent dollar builds equity—for them.

Where we talk about "leaving the hood,"
but never talk about owning the block.

If we don't own the land,
we don't control the future.

We'll just be permanent renters in someone else's America.

The Solution – Land, Legacy, and the Long Game

1. Form the Land Trust: Not Just Buying, But Protecting

A land trust is a legal shield.
It's how they protect Central Park.
How churches keep their land tax-free for 200 years.
How billionaires buy up farmland with zero exposure.

We can do it too.

Use a community land trust to own property as a group

The trust protects land from resale, seizure, or internal drama

Families lease the land (99-year leases) but the trust owns it

No flipping allowed—just roots

It's how we stop the "sellout" spiral
before it starts.

2. The "3 House Rule": Cooperative Wealth-Building

Instead of 10 people buying 10 homes solo…
10 people buy 3 properties together:

One rental (pays for the mortgage)

One flip (funds future deals)

One primary residence (for a family in need)

Everyone gets:

Shared equity

Monthly cash flow

Financial literacy from real experience

Legacy-building stories to pass down

You don't need rich friends.
You need focused ones.

3. Generational Titles & Death-Proof Paperwork

We lose billions in heir property losses every decade.

Why?

Because we don't:

Write wills

Set up transfer-on-death deeds

Assign durable power of attorney

Teach our kids how to handle probate court

Our land gets stuck in limbo.
Our families argue.
The courts feast.

But with a simple will,
a land trust, and a "no sale" clause,
we make sure the dirt stays Black—even when we're not here to defend it.

4. Sacred Land Fund + Community Exit Clauses

Every member in the sovereign community contributes to a Sacred Land Fund:

Used to buy surrounding land

Create buffer zones from gentrification

Secure farmland, wells, and natural resources

This land is:

Never for sale

Guarded by the community's spiritual and economic laws

The burial ground of ancestors, stories, and vision

We also create exit clauses:

If a member wants to leave, they must sell to the community—not outsiders

Price is fair market minus stewardship fee (to reward those who stayed)

You can leave the land.
But the land never leaves the family.

Closing Lesson – Wealth Is Not Loud. It's Rooted.

They convinced us to trade diamonds for dirt.
To wear our wealth instead of build it.
To treat land like a burden instead of the birthright it is.

But now we see it.

Wealth isn't what you hold in your hand.
It's what your grandchildren stand on.

The shade of trees you'll never sit under.
The silence of bills they'll never pay.
The power of land they can never be pushed off of again.

That's what we're building.

Not to flex.
But to fortify.

Chapter 19

Food as Freedom: Sovereign Farming, Herbal Medicine, and Breaking Grocery Store Dependency

Opening Story – The Garden That Fed Three Generations

Before the corner store… there was Grandma's yard.
Collards. Turnips. Tomatoes. Peppers.
She didn't call it "organic."
She just called it dinner.

When times got hard, she didn't panic.
She pulled from the earth.
When her blood pressure spiked, she didn't reach for pills.
She boiled leaves passed down from her grandmother.

The medicine was grown.
The food was power.
And every lesson she whispered was a survival code.

But over time, those gardens disappeared.
Fast food replaced the fields.
And we traded nourishment for convenience.

Now?

Our kids don't know what real strawberries taste like.
And we wonder why the village feels sick.

Psychological Breakdown – How Dependency Was Engineered Into Our Plates

They taught us the supermarket was "civilized."

That growing your own food meant you were poor or behind.
They shamed farming—after centuries of enslaving us to do it.
Then repackaged agriculture as "agri-business" and sold it back with a profit.

We began trusting packages over plants.
Chemicals over culture.
Microwaves over medicine.

But deep in our DNA,
we remember the soil.

The trauma runs deep—because so does the healing.
When you control your food,
you control your fear.

Corporate POV vs Street POV

Corporate Food Industry:

Prioritizes shelf life over soul

Uses GMOs, preservatives, and addictive sugars to engineer cravings

Designs grocery layouts to push high-profit garbage up front

Sells $30 “detox kits” while funding fast food chains in low-income areas

Buys up farmland and bans seed saving through lobbying

Street-Level Survival:

Relies on EBT and corner stores to make it through the week

Buys cheap food that fills the belly but empties the body

Treats diet-related illness as "normal" and unavoidable

Often resists farming because it "feels like slavery"

Lacks access to land, tools, or generational food knowledge

But here's the truth:

Growing your own food is not slavery.
It's sovereignty.

The Concern – If They Feed You, They Can Poison You

Think about it:

They ban seeds but sell pills

They own water rights but spray pesticides

They ship fake eggs and bleach meat but call it "regulation"

They build "food deserts" then blame your health on culture

They own the farms.
They own the labs.
They own the shelves.

Which means they own your lifespan,
your immune system,

your blood pressure,
your mental focus.

And if they own your food?
They own your future.

The Solution – Grow, Heal, and Reclaim the Plate

1. The Community Food Grid

Every sovereign village must establish a food grid:

Four corner gardens around the community (North, South, East, West)

One greenhouse hub for herbs, year-round crops, and plant starts

Rotating crop schedule to support soil health and diversify nutrition

Monthly planting events that double as community ceremonies

Each family:

Gets a starter plot or shared access

Receives training from elders or a certified herbalist/farmer

Puts in labor, not just lip service

This becomes our defense system.

Not just from hunger, but from corporate control.

2. The Medicine Cabinet is in the Dirt

Modern medicine is a trillion-dollar hustle.
But the real healing still grows wild:

Mullein for the lungs

Dandelion root for the liver

Nettle for allergies

Ashwagandha for stress

Soursop, burdock, elderberry, moringa — our ancestral arsenal

Every sovereign household:

Learns 10 core herbs and how to prepare them

Keeps a "living apothecary" — a section of their yard or indoor grow

Trains children on which plant helps which pain

Documents recipes from elders before they're lost

We stop treating nature as decoration
and remember she was always our doctor.

3. Grocery Liberation Strategy

We don't start by boycotting every store.
We start by replacing 1 item at a time.

Replace boxed tea with real leaves

Replace snack cakes with dried fruit and honey

Replace cow's milk with oat, almond, or coconut you made

Replace store greens with 2 rows of collards in a kiddie pool

Replace pills with herbal tinctures and sun-grown minerals

Eventually:

You build a community co-op

You trade goods internally

You use food as currency and culture

Until one day,
you walk into the grocery store…

… and realize you don't need it.

Closing Lesson – The Revolution Starts in Your Backyard

There's power in planting a seed.
It's an act of rebellion.
Of memory.
Of survival.

Your ancestors worked the land under whips.
You now work it with vision.

They bled into the soil.
You feed your children from it.

They were punished for picking.
You are sovereign for planting.

We're not just building a garden.
We're rebuilding the immune system of a people.

Food is not just fuel.
It's a mirror.

And what we put on the plate
reflects how deeply we love ourselves.

Chapter 20

The Health Trap: How the System Profits Off Our Sickness and Fears

Opening Story – The Doctor's Visit That Changed Nothing

Jameel was 34.
Worked 50 hours a week.
Stayed tired.
Had heartburn.
Was gaining weight.
Couldn't sleep without weed or pills.

He finally took a day off and went to the doctor.

In 12 minutes he walked out with:

A prescription for acid reflux

A warning about diabetes

And a suggestion to "cut back on fried foods"

That's it.

No blood panel.
No vitamin scan.
No food conversation.
No mental health screening.

But they billed his insurance $542.
And gave him 2 bottles he couldn't pronounce.

He wasn't healed.

He was processed.

Just like the chicken he ate last night.

Psychological Breakdown – Why We've Been Trained to Fear Sickness But Not Prevent It

We fear illness more than we value wellness.
Because they trained us that "health" is something you go get—
From a building, from a bottle, from a stranger in a lab coat.

They medicalized survival.
And commodified the cure.

Instead of teaching balance, they sold us panic.
Instead of root causes, they taught us reaction culture.

So we:

Don't ask what's in the food

Don't ask how emotions affect digestion

Don't ask what trauma lives in our blood

We just want the fix.
The quick one.
The paid one.

But healing has never been sold.
It's been practiced.

Corporate POV vs Street POV

Corporate Health Machine:

Sells fear first: "Get this scan, take this test, you might be dying."

Pushes pills without healing the root

Builds hospitals in poor neighborhoods after generations of toxicity

Sells insurance that covers treatment, but not prevention

Ties healthcare to jobs—so no work means no access

Street-Level Reality:

Avoids the doctor due to bills, shame, or past disrespect

Normalizes pain and fatigue as "getting old" or "just stress"

Leans on weed, alcohol, sex, or sugar to escape discomfort

Uses ER as primary care

Distrusts the system because it never taught—it just billed

They don't want you to understand your body.
Because when you do?
You cost them money.

The Concern – Sick People Don't Start Revolutions

The system is smart.

It knows:

A tired man won’t organize.

A sick woman won’t march.

A family full of processed food and side effects won’t question authority.

So they create predictable cycles:

Feed you garbage

Deny you knowledge

Blame your culture

Then sell you relief

It's slavery.
Just with pharmaceutical chains instead of iron ones.

And we pay for it every month—
Through premiums, copays, and funerals.

The Solution – Reclaiming Our Healing Tools and Systems

1. The Sovereign Clinic Model

Every sovereign community needs its own wellness center, designed not just to respond to sickness, but to teach how to prevent it.

Services include:

Nutritional coaching based on ancestral diets

Blood panel testing to identify deficiencies

Mental health and trauma release practices

Spiritual care alongside physical

Herbal medicine alongside modern tools

Staffed by:

Trained Black herbalists

Licensed practitioners aligned with truth

Elders who pass down traditional healing

Community health workers—not corporate proxies

Every child learns how the body works.
Every adult learns how to maintain it.
And every elder is respected as a healer, not hidden away.

2. The Health Curriculum We Never Got

Sovereign villages must reeducate ourselves:

Topics that get taught:

What inflammation is, how it works, and how to reduce it

The gut-brain connection (mood, food, and poop)

Signs of vitamin and mineral deficiency

Fasting cycles and detox rituals

Emotional health: How grief, stress, and unspoken trauma weaken the immune system

These become weekly teachings, not side talks.
Shared at community dinners.
Printed on walls.
Preached like gospel.

Because information is immunity.

3. Emergency Without the ER

We also build an internal urgent care system, so nobody suffers while "waiting until Monday."

Options include:

Certified first responders in each housing zone

Natural emergency remedies stocked in homes (charcoal, cayenne, garlic, etc.)

WhatsApp or Signal groups for real-time health alerts

Paid health stewards on call for minor injuries and acute symptoms

Community CPR, wound care, and child fever response training

No more watching grandma stroke out while waiting on the ambulance.
No more men ignoring chest pain because they can't afford the visit.

Health becomes ours again.

Closing Lesson – You Can't Heal in a System That Profits Off Your Pain

We've been conditioned to believe sickness is normal.
That fatigue is age.
That obesity is just "big-boned."
That medication is the only answer.

But that's a setup.

Because a people too sick to fight
is a people too weak to change.

But we remember the healing.

In the teas our grandmothers made.

In the sweats our grandfathers took.

In the fasting, the prayer, the laughter, and the land.

Our healing is not Western.
It's ancestral.
It's daily.
And it's ours.

We're not just surviving anymore.
We're remembering how to thrive.

And this time,
we write the prescription.

Chapter 21

Death Insurance: How Black Grief Became an Industry

Opening Story – Auntie's Final Debt

Aunt Brenda was the glue of the family.
Kept birthday cards in a shoebox.
Fed everyone when food stamps ran out.
Took in her sister's kids when the state came knocking.

She passed at 61.
No savings.
No will.
No plan.

Within 6 hours, the family chat lit up:

"GoFundMe coming soon"

"Anybody got connections at the funeral home?"

"She got insurance?"

"We gone need white doves, though."

By the end of the week, they raised $9,200.
Spent $8,700 on her funeral.
Nobody asked why a box and a plot cost more than her rent.

They buried Aunt Brenda in gold-trim caskets
but nobody buried the cycle.

Psychological Breakdown – Grief, Guilt, and the Performative Pressure of Death

Death is sacred.
But we've been taught to consume it, not process it.

We perform it:

Suits for the dead more expensive than what they wore alive

Paid doves and rented limos to signal love

Crying harder for Facebook than for God

It's not grief.
It's guilt, dressed in silk.

Because we know deep down:

We didn't visit enough

We didn't check in enough

We didn't build the systems to prevent this outcome

So we buy relief.
We rent honor.
We print t-shirts.
We call it closure.

But nothing closed.
Because we never opened the conversations that matter while they were alive.

Corporate POV vs. Street POV

Corporate Funeral Industry:

Packages death like a wedding: caskets, flowers, "final look" options

Charges $6K–$15K minimum for burial

Pushes pre-need insurance plans that expire or vanish

Partners with churches to build trust while upselling

Knows grief is a shortcut to spending with no resistance

Street-Level Reality:

Leans on GoFundMe and fish fries to bury loved ones

Buys burial insurance with confusing fine print

Has more memorial shirts than financial plans

Overpays for spectacle while under-planning for legacy

Treats life insurance as optional until it's too late

The industry banks on two things:
Black love and Black unpreparedness.

The Concern – We Die Without Plans and Live Without Protection

Death is the one guarantee.
But in our communities, it's the most neglected conversation.

And the most profitable one, too—
Just not for us.

We're:

Not taught estate law

Not shown how to protect land

Not trained to pass assets quietly

Not given a blueprint for dignified death without debt

We bury loved ones in gold.
But leave no gold behind.

We say "rest in peace,"
But peace didn't pay the funeral bill.
Visa did.

The Solution – Legacy Over Luxury

1. Mandatory Life Insurance in Sovereign Villages

Every adult over 18 must be taught and assisted in getting:

A simple term life insurance policy (10–20 year minimum)

A designated beneficiary within the community

A backup will with notarized copy stored internally

Quarterly education on insurance traps, fine print, and scams

Sovereign villages negotiate as a block to get group rates.

No more $89/month policies with loopholes.
No more silence.
No more GoFundMe as our emergency plan.

2. The Living Will & Legacy Lab

We create an internal office that guides every member through:

Writing wills

Naming guardians

Assigning power of attorney

Passing property with protection from probate

Teaching children how to carry legacy, not just bury it

Families are assigned Legacy Coaches,
just like life coaches—
But their job is to make sure your name don't get erased when you go.

3. Cultural Shift: Celebrating Life While People Are Still Alive

We reverse the emotional imbalance.

Give flowers while they can smell them

Film interviews with elders before they're gone

Have quarterly "Appreciation Circles" where community members honor each other in life

Create a “Time Vault” of voice recordings, letters, and wisdom to be opened upon death

That’s how you immortalize a people.
Not with marble, but with memory and message.

4. Community Funeral Fund & Burial Alternatives

Sovereign villages create an internal Emergency Burial Fund, funded monthly by all adults.

It covers:

Basic burial costs (if needed)

Dignified cremation (if preferred)

Transportation and ceremony

Immediate support for grieving family

We also establish:

Our own cemetery co-op on shared land

Green burials that are cheaper, eco-conscious, and spiritually aligned

Cremation savings funds to avoid debt-driven delays

We stop overpaying for caskets that rot.
And start honoring souls that built the village.

Closing Lesson – Legacy Is Built Before Death, Not During the Funeral

The death industry will keep profiting.
They have brochures, silk gloves, and funeral homes on every corner.

But we now build something else:

A legacy office in every sovereign village

A burial fund that doesn't exploit grief

A culture that celebrates life while we live it

A generation that teaches their children what to do when we're gone

We stop pretending death ain't coming.
We stop panicking when it knocks.
We meet it with grace, order, and memory.

Because a people who control how they die
finally learn how to control how they live.

And from this point forward,
our name don't die when we do.

Chapter 22

Welfare Dependency: When Help Becomes a Hidden Lease

Opening Story – Section 8, Section Stuck

Keisha was brilliant.
Ran her house like a CEO.
Woke up at 5, kids dressed and fed by 6, bus stop at 6:30.
EBT got them through the month, Section 8 kept the rent locked.
And every dollar she made over the limit, they took it from the voucher.

So she worked off the books.
Cleaned hair in the kitchen.
Sold plates on Fridays.
Braided edges with one hand while stirring spaghetti with the other.

But when her son won a private school scholarship, she hesitated.
If she moved, she'd lose her voucher.
If she made more, they'd cut the food.
If she started a business, they'd disqualify her.

She wasn't lazy.
She was leased.

Not to a landlord—
But to a system that charged her freedom for survival.

Psychological Breakdown – The Trap of Gratitude Over Growth

Welfare was sold to us as help.
A safety net.
A lifeline.

But over time, it turned into a leash.
One that tightens the moment you try to climb.

The system trains you to:

Fear more income

Hide your hustle

Keep your address

Limit your dreams

Quiet your ambition

It's a system built on survival shame.
Because you're punished for growing, but blamed for staying stuck.

So we become grateful for what kills us slow.

Corporate POV vs Street POV

Corporate Welfare Logic:

"We provide support" = We control outcomes

Keeps you in government housing but never builds ownership

Rewards compliance, punishes ambition

Designed to expire but structured to entrap

Runs on metrics: How many stayed poor, not how many escaped

Street-Level Reality:

Learns to "play the system" to survive

Avoids legal work to keep benefits

Stays in place because growth means risk

Builds under-the-table side hustles that can't scale

Feels guilt for wanting more

The system gives you just enough to eat,
but never enough to leave the table.

The Concern – A People Who Rely on Help Will Never Own the Land

Welfare is not inherently evil.
But it becomes evil when it punishes healing.

If our food, rent, and healthcare all depend on an outside force—
we don't own our bodies, our homes, or our options.

That's how empires neuter resistance:
by feeding you crumbs and calling it care.

The real goal of the welfare-industrial complex isn't empowerment.

It's containment.

If your benefits are at risk,
so is your willingness to rebel.

The Solution – Replacing Dependency with Cooperative Wealth

1. Sovereign Welfare Exit Strategy

Every community member who joins the sovereign village is given a three-tier plan:

Tier 1: Survival

Access to food programs, emergency housing, and temporary financial support

Community-funded rather than government-sourced

Tier 2: Stability

In-house job training, child care, elder care, and side hustle acceleration

Rent is based on contribution, not paperwork

Tier 3: Sovereignty

Land ownership options, home building, personal business launches

Health insurance and benefits via village-owned co-ops

The goal is not shame.
The goal is graduation.

From needing help…
to becoming the help.

2. Internal Assistance Without Internal Chains

The sovereign model creates its own version of "welfare," but it's reciprocal:

You get support only if you contribute in labor, wisdom, or time

Instead of ID cards, you have community credits

Instead of waiting rooms, we have solution boards

Instead of audits, we use peer-led responsibility groups to track commitment

We don't just feed you.
We build with you.

3. Replace Government Rent With Community Ownership

Instead of Section 8 or public housing, we:

Build tiny home units and multi-family dwellings owned by the village

Allow residents to rent-to-own using community contribution

Offer sweat equity options: fix a roof, build a porch, earn equity

Create internal property titles tracked by the Council

You don’t have to lie about income.
You don’t have to fake poverty to stay.
You grow—and your home grows with you.

4. Universal Contribution = Dignity

Everyone gives.
Everyone eats.
That’s the system.

A 75-year-old elder can provide wisdom, tutoring, or oral history

A 15-year-old teen can deliver meals, mentor kids, clean shared spaces

A disabled member can answer phone calls, schedule shifts, or translate documents

No one is “too broken” to contribute.
And no one is seen as a drain.

We restore dignity to aid.
We kill the shame.
And we kill the leash.

Closing Lesson – Help Without a Plan Is Just a Delay

You can’t heal in a system that needs you broken.

You can’t rise in a house that penalizes elevation.

Welfare was supposed to be a bridge.
They turned it into a maze.
But we don’t wait for permission anymore.

We:

Build our own bridges

Track our own steps

Heal our own people

And teach our children that true help comes with freedom, not paperwork

The new welfare is wealth in family, food, function, and future.

And this time,
we ain't signing their lease.

We're writing our own deed.

Chapter 23

Internal Security: How We Police Ourselves Without Becoming the Oppressor

Opening Story – The Brother They Called a Threat

His name was Romell.
Former felon.
Six years inside.
Came home quiet, humble, focused.

He didn't want trouble.
He wanted peace.
He wanted to protect what he never had—stability.

So when a fight broke out at the community garden over someone stealing tomatoes, Romell stepped in.
Calm voice. Open palms. Kept it from escalating.

But when the outsiders showed up—blue lights flashing—they didn't ask questions.
Didn't assess the situation.
Just saw a Black man with muscle and record and authority.

They threw him on the ground.
Split his lip.
And the community stood frozen—watching the very man who kept the peace get punished for protecting it.

That was the last time Romell broke up a fight.
From then on, he kept his mouth shut.
The system had trained him too.

Even peace is a threat if it doesn't come with a badge.

Psychological Breakdown – Authority Is a Trigger Word for the Oppressed

To be policed is to be stalked.
To be watched before you're understood.
To be punished for existing loudly.

Black people don't just fear the police.
We fear the idea of control without love.

Because the badge has never loved us.
It doesn't correct—it commands.
It doesn't mentor—it monitors.
It doesn't protect—it provokes.

So when we talk about self-policing, the trauma flares.
We've been beaten too long to accept discipline with open arms.

But if we don't create internal accountability,
we import outside destruction.

Corporate POV vs Street POV

Corporate Policing Model:

Invests in militarized equipment, not relationships

Hires officers from outside the community they patrol

Tracks crime, but not trauma

Prioritizes image over healing

Teaches compliance, not restoration

Street-Level Reality:

Learns to handle beef privately, often violently

Distrusts all forms of authority—especially Black ones wearing uniforms

Has no restorative justice channels, just revenge or silence

Mislabels accountability as snitching

Fears judgment more than death

So we live unprotected in two ways:

From them…

And from us.

The Concern – No Peace Without Order, No Order Without Ownership

A community that can't handle its own chaos will always be ruled from the outside.

And outside rulers bring:

Disrespect

Death

Deportation (jail is modern exile)

And dollars stolen from our schools and given to their stations

If we don't build internal systems of protection, we invite surveillance.
If we don't manage harm, we normalize it.

A sovereign village must have:

Boundaries

Watchfulness

Protection

Compassion

And enforcement with dignity

Not to punish.
But to preserve.

The Solution – Building Internal Security Without Replicating Oppression

1. The Peace Force: Not Cops. Guardians.

Each sovereign village forms a Peace Force, not a police squad.

Requirements:

Must be from the community or vetted through it

Must complete trauma-informed de-escalation training

Must be emotionally stable, not just physically capable

Must wear no weapons unless absolutely necessary

Must rotate duties to prevent power addiction

Their job is not to dominate.
It's to protect the flow of peace.

They walk with respect, not threat.
They settle, not incite.
They know the children by name.
They know the elders by face.

And their first tool is not force.
It's relationship.

2. The Council of Fire – Tiered Justice

All disputes, crimes, and harms are handled through three tiers:

Tier 1: Minor offenses (verbal disrespect, late tasks, neglect)

Handled by peer discussion circles with mediators

Resolutions involve apology, recommitment, or temporary exclusion from privilege

Tier 2: Moderate offenses (theft, property damage, verbal threats)

Brought to the Council of Fire – a mix of elders, youth, and neutral parties

Resolutions may include community service, restitution, or structured rehabilitation

Tier 3: Serious harm (violence, sexual abuse, betrayal of sovereignty)

Triggeres full investigation

If proven, can lead to long-term exile, community jury trials, or outside legal action if unavoidable

We don't tolerate predators.
But we also don't treat broken people like trash.

We weigh the heart, not just the headline.

3. The Watch System – Eyes of Respect

Every community quadrant has trained Watchers:

They're not spies.

They're respected observers.

They check on the elders.

They break up drama with wisdom.

They're trained in CPR, self-defense, and response strategy.

These Watchers are rotated, reviewed, and retrained.

So power never gets stale.
And safety never

Chapter 24

Healing the Men: Brotherhood Over Bravado

Opening Story – The Fight That Wasn't About the Fight

Two brothers almost came to blows in the garden.

One was mad about a borrowed tool.
The other was mad about something deeper—but he couldn't name it.
You could see it in his jaw.
In the way he gripped the rake like it was a weapon, not a tool.
In the way he raised his voice over something small but heavy.

What he really wanted to say was:
"Why wasn't my father around?"
"Why did prison become my rite of passage?"
"Why does peace feel like weakness?"

But none of that came out.
Only shouting.
Until an elder put his arm between them, not with force—but with presence.

He didn't yell.
Didn't threaten.
He just said:

"We all came here to unlearn the whip, son. Don't wear it now."

Psychological Breakdown – The Armor of Hurt

Most men don’t speak about their pain.
They compete with it.
Flex over it.
Or collapse under it quietly.

We're not raised to heal.
We're raised to hide.

And hiding makes us dangerous.
Not just to others—but to ourselves.

What we call “manhood” has often just been a mask for trauma.

We grew up with rules like:

Don’t cry

Don’t snitch

Don’t hug

Don’t talk about it

Don’t let ‘em see you weak

So when we feel unloved, we isolate.
When we feel attacked, we escalate.
When we feel small, we self-destruct loudly.

This is not masculinity.
This is inherited pain marketing itself as pride.

Corporate POV vs Street POV

Corporate Masculinity Model:

Work hard, shut up, retire early

Provide financially, die emotionally

Compete at all costs—even if it kills your peace

Avoid therapy, it's "for the weak"

Define manhood by title, not character

Street Masculinity Model:

Be feared, not respected

Solve conflict with fists or fire

Get money fast, by any means

Have multiple women, trust none

Cry in silence, die with secrets

Both models reward performance, not processing.
Neither model teaches internal repair.

So men walk around angry, guarded, explosive—
And we wonder why brotherhood keeps breaking.

The Concern – A Community of Broken Men Becomes a Battlefield

If men don't heal, they become hidden enemies of the peace they claim to protect.

Unhealed men:

Sabotage relationships

Compete with their brothers

Disrespect their elders

Mistreat women

Distrust joy

Destroy opportunity

Unhealed men don't build—they hoard.
Don't love—they possess.
Don't lead—they dominate.

So we can't build sovereign systems without addressing the sickness sitting inside many of our brothers.

Because freedom without emotional literacy is still a prison.

The Solution – Building a Brotherhood That Heals in Public, Not Just in Private

1. Rituals of Release

Monthly gatherings called "Circle of Smoke"

A fire is lit.

No phones. No recording.

Just men. Just truth.

Each man speaks what he's been carrying—anger, guilt, shame, failure.

No one interrupts. No one fixes. We hold space.

Then the group decides together:

Does this man need help?

Does he need correction?

Does he need a break from responsibility to realign?

We don't exile men for hurting.
We walk them back into their higher self—together.

2. Fatherhood Apprenticeships

Elders are paired with younger men not to preach—but to listen.

Each pair commits to:

One weekly walk

One shared project

One deep conversation per month

The goal is to rebuild emotional modeling—
not through lectures, but through living example.

This fills the gaps of fatherlessness and restores generational masculine intelligence.

3. Accountability Panels

Every 90 days, men are reviewed by:

Their peers

Their apprentices or sons

Their partners (if applicable)

They're asked:

Are you dependable?

Are you present?

Are you disciplined?

Are you honest?

Are you healing?

This is not punishment.
It's ritualized reflection.

It keeps ego in check.
And makes healing part of leadership, not separate from it.

Closing Lesson – Power is Nothing if the Soul is Still Bleeding

The goal isn't soft men.
It's sovereign men.

Men who can:

Hold their rage without leaking it

Hold their families with presence

Hold themselves accountable before anyone else does

A healed man doesn't need to dominate.
He doesn't need to compete with love.
He doesn't fear his own softness.
Because he knows softness doesn't kill masculinity—
it completes it.

This isn't therapy.
This is survival through evolution.

We don't heal just for us.
We heal because the next generation is watching how we carry what we weren't given.

And if we don't teach them different,
they'll inherit our wounds as tradition.

Housing Sovereignty: From RV Camps to Built Homes

Opening Story – The Trailer That Became a Temple

When Malik moved into the community, he didn't get a house.
He got an old RV, stripped and cleaned, parked in the singles' section.
Four walls, thin insulation, no luxury.
But it was his.

That RV gave him a bed without eviction notices.
A fridge without stolen food.
A lock without landlords.

Six months later, Malik was leading a crew—building modular units for families.
By year two, his RV was gone, and a duplex stood in its place.
Malik kept the keys to his first RV, though.
Not as a symbol of poverty.
But as proof of process:
You start where you can.
You end where you build.

Psychological Breakdown – Why Housing Feels Like a Prison or a Dream

For us, housing has always been trauma.

Redlined out of neighborhoods.

Section 8 capped our ceilings.

Gentrification pushed us out of our own blocks.

Developers used zoning like a whip.

So when we hear "housing," we feel two extremes:
Luxury or loss.

We were never taught the middle ground:
flexible, layered, community-based housing that grows as we grow.

The truth?
You don't need marble countertops to be free.
You need ownership, security, and expansion.

Corporate POV vs. Street POV

Corporate Housing Industry:

Pushes mortgages as “wealth,” while trapping families in 30-year chains

Profits off eviction cycles

Buys foreclosures and resells them at inflated prices

Uses zoning to block low-cost solutions like tiny homes or mobile units

Keeps the housing market intentionally scarce

Street-Level Reality:

Rents apartments forever, often with no lease protection

Stacks families into overcrowded spaces

Treats housing as temporary—never generational

Avoids paperwork because systems exploit the unprepared

Builds homes out of hustle, not blueprint

Both sides leave us vulnerable.
Either to debt…
Or to displacement.

The Concern – If We Don’t Build Housing Systems, We’ll Be Tenants in Our Own Village

You can’t build sovereignty if your shelter is shaky.

If every storm floods your trailer…
If every paycheck controls whether the lights stay on…
If every landlord can uproot you with a letter…

… then you don't own your future.

And in a sovereign village, we can't afford to let outsiders own our walls.

We must create layered housing models—
affordable, adaptable, and resistant to foreclosure or seizure.

The Solution – Housing Sovereignty Blueprint

1. Layered Housing Tiers

Not everyone enters the same way.
So we build a structure where housing meets life stage and capacity:

RV Camps for Singles
Affordable starter units with shared kitchens, bathrooms, and power hubs.
Dignity restored, discipline built.

Single & Double-Wides
Great for small families, affordable to install, easily upgraded.

Triple-Wides & Modular Homes
Anchor housing for larger families or long-term residents.

Built Homes
Reserved for elders, leaders, and generational families.
Brick, earthbag, or modular cube homes built to last.

Quadplexes
Transitional housing for couples, new families, or returning members.

Every unit is not just shelter.
It's a stage of sovereignty.

2. Sweat Equity Housing Program

Nobody moves in for free.
Every house is earned by contribution.

Build hours = reduced rent

Maintenance service = equity credit

Labor on other people's homes = credit toward your own

This way, every nail hammered is not just work.
It's ownership.

3. Shared Utilities for Sustainability

Instead of every unit having its own bills:

Central solar grids feed multiple homes

Water wells and catchment systems shared across zones

Laundry centers reduce cost and stress on infrastructure

This lowers costs, raises efficiency, and keeps money in-house.

4. No Outside Landlords. Ever.

The land trust owns everything.
Members don't pay "rent."
They pay contribution dues—which recycle into infrastructure, repairs, and expansion.

This eliminates eviction as punishment.
Disputes are settled by council, not court.

The home is sacred, not speculative.

Closing Lesson – A Roof Without Roots Is Still Homelessness

Housing sovereignty isn't about granite counters or square footage.
It's about freedom from eviction.
It's about building homes that grow with families.
It's about sweat equity—turning labor into legacy.

Because we can't call ourselves sovereign if we're still tenants in someone else's empire.

Our homes are not rentals.
They are temples of survival.
They are monuments of work.
And they are the proof that we'll never be uprooted again.

Chapter 25

Transportation & Fleet Power: How Vehicles Become Tools of Sovereignty

Opening Story – When Wheels Became Wings

Tyrese used to walk three miles to work.
Then he'd catch a ride to pick up groceries for his grandmother.
When it rained, he wrapped his shoes in plastic bags and kept walking.

In the city, his car got towed over unpaid tickets.
In the country, no bus route came within 15 miles.
Transportation was no longer a tool.
It was a trap.

Then he joined the community.
Didn't have to buy a car.
Didn't have to lease a lemon.

Instead, he signed up for the internal driver registry.
Picked a schedule.
Maintained the van.
And became one of the fleetmen—paid weekly to keep the community mobile.

By year's end, he had driven elders to clinic checkups,
helped single moms get groceries,
and delivered tools to a home repair site.

He wasn't a driver anymore.
He was a pillar of movement.

Psychological Breakdown – Why a Car Isn't Just a Car

In our world, mobility is access.

And access is power.

But when you're poor, transportation becomes a psychological weight:

Missed interviews because the bus was late

DMV hoops just to prove your name is your name

Loans at 24% APR for cars with cracked engines

A broken car becomes a broken life plan

When you can't move, your world shrinks.
And when your world shrinks, your dreams follow.

Transportation trauma is real.
Especially for those who've never had reliable wheels.

So we must stop treating vehicles as luxury symbols.
And start treating them as strategic tools of freedom.

Corporate POV vs Street POV

Corporate Transportation Industry:

Pushes overpriced cars to poor buyers through predatory loans

Sells image instead of function (luxury over utility)

Ties car ownership to credit, creating debt loops

Uses planned obsolescence to force replacements

Penalizes the poor with high insurance and fines

Street Transportation Reality:

Rideshare dependency drains cash

Buying "cash cars" with hidden engine issues

No maintenance knowledge, no warranty protection

No titles, constant registration problems

Using unreliable transportation to chase stable income

Both models trap us.
One through image worship, the other through survival mode.

Neither offers long-term transportation sovereignty.

The Concern – Without Our Own Wheels, We Move on Their Terms

Imagine building a self-sufficient community...
…but having to leave it to work because you have no van.
Or not being able to transport goods because nobody has a truck.
Or relying on government medical vans to take elders to the doctor.

That’s not sovereignty.
That’s dependency in motion.

You can't protect what you can't reach.
You can't grow what you can't transport.
You can't empower who can't get around.

If we don't build a fleet system,
we'll build a village with no circulation.

And anything without circulation?
Dies.

The Solution – Sovereign Fleet Infrastructure

1. The Fleet Strategy: Bulk, Function, Reliability

Buy 200+ used work trucks, cargo vans, and multipurpose vehicles in bulk under the community LLC.

Target models:

Ford F-150 / F-250

Chevy Silverado / Express Vans

Toyota Tacomas / Tundras

Nissan NV / Frontier Work Vans

Years: 2019–2021 preferred.
Low mileage. Clean titles. Maintenance records mandatory.

Negotiate fleet rates with overwhelmed dealerships.
Pay cash or through pooled funding.
Use community mechanics for all repairs.

2. Internal Transportation Roles

Establish core transportation jobs:

Fleet Drivers (rotating shifts, licensed, vetted)

Maintenance Crew (certified or trained in-house)

Logistics Coordinators (scheduling, fuel, repair logs)

Transport Dispatchers (track trips, emergencies, supply runs)

This builds jobs + mobility.

3. Strategic Use of Vehicles

Each vehicle is assigned by function, not for ego:

Food Pickup Vans (weekly grocery runs, food bank pickups)

Elder Transport (clinic rides, mobile wheelchair access)

Tool & Supply Haulers (construction, repair, storage)

Youth Shuttle Vans (education, events, field trips)

Security Patrol Units (day/night community perimeter checks)

Emergency Vehicles (first aid kits, backup comms)

No one “owns” the vehicle.
We own the outcome of shared mobility.

4. Member Access Without Ownership

Single members can:

Join a driver pool

Rent by hour or day through internal credit

Earn priority access through labor or training

No Uber. No dependency. No isolation.

We move together, or we don't move at all.

Closing Lesson – Movement is Memory, and Freedom Requires Both

Our ancestors walked miles to freedom.
So it's not about having fancy wheels.
It's about building a system that ensures no one is left behind.

A sovereign people must:

Build their own roads

Control their own wheels

Move on their own time

Because if we can't control how we move,
we don't control how we grow.

And in a system designed to trap us in place—
movement is the greatest rebellion.

Chapter 26

The Animals Are Assets: What We Raise, How We Eat, and Why It Matters

Opening Story – The Chicken That Changed Everything

Kamaya was nine when she helped deliver her first baby goat.

She thought animals were just background noise—smelly, loud, pointless.
Until one day, her community ran out of eggs.

The store nearby was closed.
The trucks hadn't delivered.
The shelves were empty.

That morning, Kamaya fed the chickens.
By noon, six brown eggs sat in her basket.

She didn't just carry breakfast.
She carried independence.

Years later, she'd grow to run the animal division of the village, managing rotations, breeding logs, feed supply, and vet care.
But it all started with one moment:
the day a chicken saved her people from hunger.

Psychological Breakdown – Animal Disconnect and Nutritional Dependence

For most of us, meat comes wrapped in plastic and foam trays.

We don't know the source, the process, or the sacrifice.
We eat what's cheap, fast, and dead already.

Why?

Because we've been programmed to fear the work of raising animals—
and romanticize the ease of buying them.

But when we lost that connection, we didn't just lose farming.
We lost sovereignty over our nutrition.

Modern Black communities have become food dependent:

Fast food over livestock

Dollar stores over co-ops

Government surplus over gardens

We were once a people who raised goats, chickens, rabbits, and tilapia in backyards.
Now we get our protein from processed, addictive, low-quality scraps.

This isn't just unhealthy.
It's psychological slavery.

Corporate POV vs Street POV

Corporate Agriculture System:

Injects animals with hormones and antibiotics

Mass-produces meat at the expense of animal health and human disease

Controls supply chains from slaughterhouse to supermarket

Uses animal agriculture to inflate prices and restrict access

Profits off hunger, not nutrition

Street-Level Perspective:

Buys meat in bulk from Walmart or corner stores

Rarely considers raising livestock

No access to fresh eggs, goat milk, or sustainable protein

Relies on SNAP, school lunches, or "survival food"

Thinks livestock is "white people farming" or "too much work"

Result?
We don't control what we eat.
We fear doing so.
And we pay in disease and dependency.

The Concern – Without Animal Systems, We Stay at the Mercy of the Grocery Store

No matter how many homes we build…
No matter how many jobs we create…

If we can't feed ourselves,
we are never free.

When the trucks stop running,
when inflation hits beef prices,
when supply chains crash,
when grocery stores ration food...

What will we do?

Will we starve in sovereign homes?
Or will we remember the old ways—
and upgrade them?

The Solution – Strategic Animal Infrastructure for a 1,000-Person Village

1. Animal Zones by Purpose and Output

We divide livestock across four focus areas:

A. Egg & Meat Poultry

Egg layers: Rhode Island Red, ISA Brown, Leghorns

Meat birds: Cornish Cross, Freedom Rangers

Rotation cycles every 6–8 weeks for broilers

Mobile coops (chicken tractors) to reduce feed cost and fertilize land

B. Dairy & Meat Goats

Breeds: Nubian (milk), Boer (meat), Nigerian Dwarf (milk + friendly for kids)

Rotational grazing

Milking stations

Goat milk = cheese, soap, medicine

C. Rabbits

Low feed cost, fast breeders

Easy to process

Great starter for youth agriculture training

D. Fish Farming (Aquaculture)

Tilapia and Catfish in contained tanks or dug ponds

Recirculating systems for indoor setups

Year-round protein source

Water reused for crop fertilization

2. Youth & Elders Animal Training System

Children assigned to animal projects: feeding, tracking births, cleaning stalls

Elders share oral traditions, healing remedies, meat preparation, hide uses

This isn't just agriculture.
It's heritage work.

3. Animal Products Economy

All animals serve multiple roles:

Eggs = breakfast + bartering item

Milk = cheese, ice cream, soap

Hides = leather for crafts

Manure = fertilizer

Feathers = pillows, insulation

Meat = sustenance + trade

We create an internal circular economy where animals produce value, not just meals.

4. Veterinary + Processing Systems

In-house veterinary team trained or contracted monthly

Scheduled deworming, disease prevention

Mobile butchering units with sterile setups

No trauma-based slaughter—ritual respect and clean technique

We control health, death, and the sacred balance of nature.

5. Security + Ethics Guidelines

No overbreeding

No factory-style suffering

No selling animals outside the community without council approval

Members are trained before handling

All systems reviewed quarterly for sustainability

The animals are not property.
They are partnership.

Closing Lesson – If You Can't Feed Your Children, You Are Still a Slave

This system isn't about becoming farmers.
It's about reclaiming a relationship with food.

A people who can't feed themselves are a people who can't free themselves.
Our ancestors fed 10 children with two goats and a coop of hens.
Now we feed 1 child with $300 worth of fast food.

That's not advancement.
That's engineered dependence.

Our animals are not decorations.
They are guardians of independence.
Every cluck, bleat, and splash is a revolution.

Because when we no longer fear feeding ourselves,
we no longer fear the system.

And that's when we truly win.

Chapter 27

Digital Power: Fiber Optics, Tech Hubs, and Controlling the Cloud

Opening Story – The Boy Who Couldn't Upload

Devin had ideas.
Brilliant ones.
He was building websites on a cracked iPad using public Wi-Fi.
Coding between shifts at the gas station.

But every time he tried to upload his latest build,
the signal dropped.
The app froze.
The connection died.

He wasn't underqualified.
He was underconnected.

One day, the community tech center opened.
Devin walked in, plugged into fiber-optic internet, and hit "upload."
That same site got him his first remote gig.
Today, Devin trains 50 teens a month.
The server room runs 24/7.
And nobody's brilliance gets blocked by bandwidth again.

Psychological Breakdown – The Poverty of the Unplugged

We think the internet is a luxury.
That fast Wi-Fi is something for gamers or influencers.
That computers are for offices, not for us.

But in the digital age, the disconnect is deadly.
If you don't control your access to tech:

You're silenced.

You're slowed.

You're locked out of innovation.

Poor Black communities have been turned into data deserts.
No fiber lines.
Slow upload speeds.
Overpriced mobile data.
Libraries with time limits.
Schools with outdated equipment.

It's not accidental.
It's engineered poverty by bandwidth.
And it stops brilliance before it blooms.

Corporate POV vs. Street POV

Corporate Tech Infrastructure:

Builds fast networks in wealthy zip codes

Charges poor areas more for slower speed

Lobbies against free municipal broadband

Monetizes user data through surveillance

Keeps tech training centralized and credential-based

Street-Level Reality:

Relies on hotspot phones or shared passwords

No access to remote work pipelines

Kids falling behind because Chromebooks don’t work without signal

Digital business dreams die in loading screens

Sees tech as "for them" not "for us"

One is plugged in and monetizing.
The other is buffering and broke.

The Concern – If We Don’t Own the Wires, We’ll Stay Trapped in Digital Poverty

You can’t build a future in the analog past.

Every system—from security to banking, from school to sales—is going digital.
If we don’t control our digital infrastructure:

Our youth stay disconnected

Our stories stay untold

Our work can’t scale

Our truth gets shadowbanned

We must stop being customers of tech
and become owners of infrastructure.

The Solution – The Sovereign Digital Stack

1. Install Internal Fiber Optic Network

Partner with ethical ISPs or install local towers

Lay fiber underground throughout the village

Central hub server room with backup generators and cooling

Decentralized Wi-Fi mesh for seamless access

Encrypted internal network for sensitive data

No reliance on Comcast or Spectrum.
We own the wires.
We control the bandwidth.

2. Build the Community Tech Center

Functions:

24/7 open hours

Remote work lab

Podcast and video editing suites

Game design and coding classes

Secure cloud backups for business files

Repair & refurbishing lab for broken tech

Youth aren't just trained to use tech.
They're trained to fix, code, and deploy it.

3. Create Digital Job Pipelines

Partner with ethical tech companies for remote gigs

In-house contracts for editing, AI tagging, e-commerce

Web design crews for external clients

App development teams trained to serve internal businesses

You’re not just online.
You’re earning online.

4. Encrypt Our Cloud and Data

Create internal cloud storage for members' records

Secure family medical info, housing data, finance logs

End-to-end encryption

Private servers owned by the community

Because you’re not sovereign if your files live on Google Drive.
Digital land is land, too.
And it must be protected.

5. Train for the Future, Not the Past

We don’t teach just typing.
We teach:

AI literacy

Blockchain security

3D modeling

Digital marketing

Drone operations

Cloud architecture

This ain't tech for tech's sake.
It's skill for survival.
And currency for independence.

Closing Lesson – The New Chains Are Invisible, But They Buffer Just the Same

The plantation of today doesn't have a field.
It has a firewall.
It doesn't beat you with whips.
It drowns you in slow speeds.

And if your brilliance can't upload,
they don't have to silence you—
they just have to disconnect you.

But when we control the signal,
we control the story.
We control the job.
We control the flow of currency, culture, and code.

And that,
in the digital age,
is true sovereignty.

Chapter 28

Why We Must Build It Now: The Future Without This Blueprint

Opening Story – The Warning of 'What If'

She sat on the porch where her grandmother used to braid her hair.
But this time, it was quiet.
No music.
No laughter.
Just boarded windows, a plastic bag dancing in the wind, and the distant hum of police sirens.

Across the street, the house where Uncle Ron taught her to box had been foreclosed and flipped.
The new owners didn't wave.
Didn't speak.
Just trimmed hedges and locked the gate.

Her people were gone.
Moved out.
Pushed out.
Locked up.
Or buried under debt, disease, and defeat.

She whispered, "What if we had built something?"
But by then, the land wasn't theirs.
And neither was the future.

Psychological Breakdown – The Grief of Potential

There's a silent grief we carry.
The grief of knowing we could've.

The regret of knowing we didn't.

This grief shows up in our bodies as stress, in our streets as violence, and in our eyes as tiredness.
Because deep down, we feel the truth:
We had time.
We had chances.
But we waited.

We kept saying:
"When I get some money."
"When the world calms down."
"When someone else does it first."

But delayed vision becomes denied survival.
And the longer we wait, the more our children inherit the collapse.

Corporate POV vs. Street POV

Corporate View:

Builds long-term plans 10–50 years out

Acquires land early, quietly

Creates scarcity, then sells access

Makes you believe survival is tied to their system

Already has off-grid bunkers, AI infrastructure, food stores

Street View:

Deals with emergencies, not strategy

Lives check-to-check, day-by-day

Doesn't trust systems, but has no system of its own

Waits for permission, then blames the game

Reacts to collapse instead of preparing for it

The result?
One side is fortified.
The other side is evicted.

The Concern – What Happens If We Don't Build Now?

Let's be blunt.
If we don't build now:

Gentrification will claim every hood and every memory

Our children will work for the same system that broke us

We'll be begging for land when it costs triple

Water, Wi-Fi, and safety will be luxuries, not rights

"Black wealth" will stay a hashtag, not a reality

All our creative gifts will fund their platforms, not our people

Death will come slowly—through processed food, loneliness, weak healthcare, and unspoken mental illness

We will leave no blueprint.
Only ashes.

The Solution – The Now Strategy

1. Take Land Seriously – Today

Pool 10–20 trusted members

Lock in rural land with water, zoning freedom, and acreage

Even 5 acres is a fortress if managed right

Stop buying what can't grow or shelter

Start with what you can afford, and build from there

2. Finalize the 10 Essential Systems

Housing

Food & Water

Security

Education

Health

Communication

Transportation

Currency

Governance

Culture

You don't need all 10 to start.
But you'll lose everything if you ignore them all.

3. Think in 20-Year Terms

Build what your child's child will inherit

Design everything to outlast you

Plant seeds you'll never see grow

Stop thinking in jobs. Start thinking in legacies.

4. Normalize the Roles of Builders

Leaders

Land Scouts

Builders

Mechanics

Farmers

Planners

Teachers

Creatives

Enforcers

Visionaries

Everyone has a place.

No one gets to be idle.
And no role is more sacred than another.

5. Protect the Culture While You Build

Document your rituals, food, phrases, and stories

Don't let them whitewash your identity as they erase your land

Keep your flags, your music, your tongue

Because what good is land if the soul that lived on it is gone?

Closing Manifesto – Tomorrow Is Already Here

This isn't about prepping.
This is about positioning.
Because the storm isn't coming — it's here.

Climate.
Surveillance.
Economic collapse.
Identity theft.
Digital control.
Cultural erasure.

They've already built bunkers.
They've already bought land.
They've already disconnected us from each other and then called it "progress."

But this book, this blueprint, this awakening—
It's your reminder that it's not too late.
It's your proof that you don't have to play their game.

It’s your strategy to stop being a casualty and start being a constructor.

So don’t just read this.
Build from it.
Copy it.
Improve it.
Localize it.
Adapt it.
And pass it on.

Because if we wait another 10 years,
we’ll be too broke, too scattered, and too gentrified to recover.

And they’ll look back at this moment
as the last time we had a chance to break the chain.

We build now—
Or we vanish forever.

CHAPTER 29 : THE LIE THAT KILLED BLACK POWER

The Collapse of Group Economics and the Rise of the Individual Trap

The Story: How We Lost Everything We Built

Before integration, we had something that most don't even realize we lost: power through self-reliance. Real power. Entire Black towns ran their own schools, clinics, farms, grocery stores, bus companies, banks, and even airplanes. Yes—planes. From Tulsa to Rosewood to Wilmington to Durham's Hayti District, Black wealth was tangible. You didn't need to beg a white man for a job—you worked for your uncle, your neighbor, your community.

Then came the lie.

The lie said, "If you can sit next to them, you're equal."

We marched, bled, and begged to be let into systems that never wanted us. The Civil Rights Movement fought to open white doors, and when those doors cracked open, we sprinted through—leaving our businesses, schools, and hospitals to rot.

Desegregation wasn't a win for Black power—it was the silent death of it.

What tanks and mobs didn't destroy in Black Wall Street, desegregation did. And here's the part most people don't know: the survivors of the 1921 Tulsa Massacre sued the city and won. Many of them rebuilt. But once integration came, Black customers took their dollars elsewhere, and the rebuilt economy died quietly. The lawsuits didn't save us—our own disloyalty did us in.

We gave up our grocery stores to shop at Piggly Wiggly. We gave up our schools to sit in classrooms with teachers who didn't want to teach us. We stopped buying Black toothpaste, Black shoes, Black eggs, and Black meat. And when the community dollars stopped circulating, those buildings got foreclosed or sold off for pennies. Many of those same blocks now sit as liquor stores, title pawn shops, or gentrified smoothie cafés.

We inherited the most powerful community-based economy ever created by oppressed people—and we sold it for ice cubes.

The Psychological Breakdown: The White Man's Ice is Colder

This chapter isn't about nostalgia—it's about brainwashing. The destruction of group economics was not just physical. It was psychological. Somewhere along the way, we started believing that white products were better. That white approval was better. That white systems were more trustworthy.

We swallowed the poison of individualism—thinking that if we could "make it out," we'd be free. But freedom isn't individual. It's collective.

"The white man's ice is colder" is more than a joke. It's a mindset of inferiority. It's why a Black man will drive across town to a white barbershop just to say he got cut in Buckhead. It's why a Black woman will trust a white doctor over a Black herbalist—even if the herbalist cured her grandmother for 30 years. It's why we don't feel successful until our skin color is the minority in the room.

The psychological warfare was complete. They didn't have to burn our stores anymore—we abandoned them ourselves.

Corporate POV vs Street POV: Ownership vs Outsourcing

Corporate POV:
In corporate America, ownership is sacred. They franchise, license, and buy in bulk. They don't care who's offended—they protect the bag. Executives don't argue about unity—they have lawyers that make unity a contract. No white CEO is worried about being "invited in." They build, hire their nephews, and block others out.

Street POV:
On the block, everybody wants to be the only one winning. Nobody wants to share the connect. You can't even get a hustler to collaborate on a food truck without beef over who owns what. We compete where we should partner. We look down on the corner store owner but buy from him every day. We'll shoot another Black man over "territory," but let foreigners own every business on that same block.

What do they have that we don't? Contracts. Trust. Vision. And the memory of war. Immigrant families come here knowing struggle. They don't forget it. We forgot. And because of that, they build empires while we rent corner stores named after other people's children.

The Concern: But What If We Can't Rebuild?

Let's be honest. Most Black people today don't know how to run a business, balance a ledger, or even grow a tomato.

It's not entirely our fault. We were raised on survival, not sovereignty. Many of us never saw a real blueprint growing up—just bills, eviction notices, and check advance loans.

So when you hear "group economics," you might think, "We ain't ready for that. We too divided. Too emotional. Too broke."

That fear is real. But it's also a lie we've been fed to keep us scared.

You don't need everybody. You need enough. Enough people with skills. Enough people willing to learn. Enough people willing to sacrifice comfort for freedom.

No revolution starts with a thousand hands. It starts with twelve apostles. A dozen Panthers. A few brave builders.

And when it comes to rebuilding Black economics—we already have the blueprint. We've done it before.

The Solution: Rebuilding Through Blueprint, Not Emotion

Step one is memory. We must remember that we built before. Durham, North Carolina was once known as "The Black Wall Street of the South." They had their own bus line. Harlem was once so booming that Malcolm X called it the "Capital of Black America." In Mississippi, the Deacons for Defense protected Black businesses with rifles and patrol cars. We didn't just dream—we executed.

Step two is structure. We can't rebuild based on vibes. We need paperwork, processes, and plans. That means forming community LLCs, creating bylaws, vetting members, investing in land, and assigning responsibility. One person grows the crops. Another secures the perimeter. Another runs the clinic. Everyone must earn their keep—through money or labor.

Step three is repetition. We need systems, not just speeches. Training in trades. Group savings plans. Joint business ownership. Co-op grocery stores. Apprenticeship programs. Every skill from farming to fiber optics must be internalized. We don't hire out what we can train in-house.

Real-World Examples of Black Group Economics (Then & Now)

Tulsa, OK (1921) – Over 600 Black-owned businesses: banks, hotels, law offices, barbershops, theaters. Burned down, rebuilt, then abandoned post-integration.

Mound Bayou, MS – Founded by formerly enslaved men. Had its own hospital, schools, bank, newspaper, and cotton gin. One of the most self-sufficient Black towns in U.S. history.

Freedom Georgia Initiative (2020) – 19 families bought 97 acres in Georgia to build a safe Black town from scratch.

Liberty Bank (Current) – One of the largest Black-owned banks in the U.S., pushing group lending programs and community reinvestment.

The Freedom Georgia Initiative (2021) – Still expanding. They created land trusts, began organizing for food sovereignty, and created member co-ops.

If we combine historic knowledge with modern tools—AI, solar, fiber optics, self-publishing, blockchain contracts—we can not only rebuild, but surpass what we once had.

The Closing Lesson

We didn't lose Black power because of poverty.
We lost it because of desire—the desire to be accepted.
Desegregation gave us access to someone else's table, and in exchange, we burned our own down.

But now the kitchen is empty. And the food is cold.

It's time to build again—not out of hate, but out of strategy. Not out of revenge, but out of memory. Because the truth is, we were never behind—we just got distracted.

Individualism is the most expensive addiction Black America has ever known. And group economics is the rehab.

The road won't be easy.
People will flake.
Some won't believe.
Some will betray.
But nothing worth building ever comes without sacrifice.

And those who fear sacrifice will always live in systems built by those who didn't.

Chapter 30: The Return to the Root – Replanting Our Economic Legacy

The Story: "The Corner Store That Never Came Back"

In 1962, a Black man named Mr. Lyles owned a corner store on the east side of town. Everyone knew him. He extended credit to the single mothers, hired the neighborhood boys in the summer, and let elders sit in the back with a cold Coke. His store was more than business — it was community. A gathering place. A lifeline.

But after desegregation, white stores opened nearby — shinier, newer, with slicker packaging. And we ran to them. Mr. Lyles couldn't compete with their cheaper prices — not because he was greedy, but because he didn't have the mass supply chains or bulk discounts. Week by week, his regulars vanished. His store closed in '69. And his building? Bought by the city for pennies and later flipped into a Starbucks.

Years later, his daughter said:

"He never blamed white folks. He blamed us. He said we didn't understand our power."

The Psychological Breakdown: "The White Man's Ice Is Colder" Syndrome

This mentality runs deep: that validation only comes from proximity to whiteness.
When Black folks saw access to white businesses, we mistook inclusion for freedom.
We abandoned our shops, clinics, banks, and schools — thinking theirs were "better."

We internalized inferiority.
We stopped seeing our people as the producers of value, and ourselves as worthy customers of our own excellence.

That syndrome wasn't just mental — it became policy. Integration wasn't just social — it was economic sabotage. The moment Black dollars stopped circulating within, our power bled out. One drip at a time.

Street POV vs. Corporate POV

Street Side:
"We gotta get it how we live."
You got barbers, braiders, hustlers, cooks, repairmen. All trying to survive off solo income. But no insurance. No HR. No retirement. Just hustle 'til your knees give out. And if someone undercuts you? It's war. There's no unity. No union. No backup.

Corporate Side:
"Protect the brand. Protect the pipeline."
Corporations train people how to work together — not just to survive, but to scale. They use HR, marketing, finance teams, legal counsel. Everyone plays a role. Nobody steps out of line. Every dollar is tracked. Every mistake is documented.
They win because they build as a unit. And they only hire insiders — not out of racism, but out of survival instinct.

The Concern: Black Individualism vs. Collective Power

We now have Black doctors, lawyers, engineers, stylists — but where's the collective infrastructure?
Where are our:

Black-owned clinics?

Black fiber-optic tech companies?

Black distribution centers?

Black-owned farmland supplying our grocery stores?

They don't exist at scale — not because we lack talent, but because we never reconnected the chain.

The Hispanic community buys buildings and rotates family income.
Asian communities pool for business capital and pass ownership generationally.
But us? We start GoFundMe campaigns alone.

The Real History: Black Wall Street Rebuilt

What they don't teach you is that after the Tulsa Massacre, survivors sued the city and won.
They rebuilt Black Wall Street again in the 1930s.

But by the 1960s, desegregation let white banks offer loans and white stores take Black customers.
By 1970, the second wave of Black Wall Street was gone.
Not burned — bought out and abandoned.

We didn't lose it once.
We lost it twice — and the second time, we handed it over with a smile.

Strategic Solution: A Blueprint for Reconnection

Mandated Group Ownership:

Require any business that operates in a Black community to be at least 51% community-owned or pay a community tax that goes to local infrastructure.

Community Guilds:
Train up trade skill networks — plumbing, HVAC, welding, coding — and contract in-house. We should never hire outsiders for services we can train our own youth to do.

Collective Capital Funds:
Like churches passed the plate, create community Roth IRAs, property pools, and emergency business loans from within. Use mobile banking tools and automatic contributions.

Asset Protection Protocol:
No property sold without 5-year approval council. If someone moves, land must stay within the collective unless every vote approves.

Black Credit Union & Internal Currency:
Build a co-op based bank and use a digital community token for internal trade and labor exchange, like modern-day "credit books" or time banks.

Final Truth:

"They told us to run from the plantation — and we ran straight into the mall."

We were never lazy. We were misled.
We were never incapable. We were under-equipped.
We were never unworthy. We were untrained in unity.

Now we return to the root — to what Mr. Lyles knew, what Black Wall Street proved, and what our future depends on:

Ownership. Unity. Obedience to the collective vision.

Because if we don't own it, we'll rent our survival forever.

Chapter 31: The Mirror Test — Can We Lead What We Build?

Narrative Story:

Jameel stood at the center of the newly cleared land, boots sunk into fresh red clay, sweat dripping from his brow as if baptizing the soil with grit. The council had just finished zoning approval for their Black-owned village, complete with permits to build tiny homes, establish a community trade school, and install solar-powered irrigation for the farms.

But something was wrong. The same brothers who rallied for freedom were now beefing over parking spaces. The finance team mismanaged the communal budget, funneling money into their side hustles. The head of security had slept with one of the married sisters in the health tent, and whispers of mistrust started to replace the chants of unity. The streets weren't invading the village — egos were.

Jameel, a man once heralded as the visionary, was now questioning if he had helped build something beautiful that we still weren't ready to lead.

And that's the real test of sovereignty.

Psychological Breakdown:

Building the village is only half the battle. The other half is governance. Not legal documents — but emotional maturity, integrity, accountability, and the ability to lead without becoming tyrannical. Many of us have been victims for so long that when we finally get a taste of power, we mimic the oppressor. We don't decolonize leadership — we repaint it Black.

We forget: oppression trains the oppressed to only see power in dominance.

This is the mirror test. Not to see if we can own land. But can we steward it? Can we make decisions that center legacy over ego? Can we correct each other without shame? Can we protect each other without acting like we own each other?

If trauma is unhealed, ownership just gives us more things to destroy.

Corporate POV vs. Street POV:

Corporate POV: In the boardroom, companies rise or fall based on leadership models. A CEO with vision but no humility ruins culture. Toxic leadership bleeds talent. That's why succession planning, accountability protocols, and quarterly reviews exist — not just for metrics, but for morale.

Street POV: In the block, the OG who held the corner with respect was replaced by the young gun who killed without principle. The rules changed, and so did the energy. Without codes, the game became chaos. Respect was replaced by fear. And you can't build anything stable on fear.

In both worlds, power without principle creates collapse.

Central Concern:

Can Black people truly sustain group economics and self-governance without replicating the very systems that harmed us?

Strategic Solution:

We need internal checks and balances — not just to protect the land, but to protect the people on the land.

Council of Accountability: Every quarter, leaders must present decisions made, funds spent, and future plans to the community — publicly. No ego protection.

Rotational Leadership: No one holds the same seat for more than 18 months without renewal. Leadership must rotate or re-earn their position by review.

Conflict Resolutions Systems: Build "peace circles" and mediation teams, trained to resolve disputes with honesty, not hierarchy.

Cultural Codes: Written and agreed-upon codes of conduct, consequences, and communication must be signed by every member. Not law — culture.

Therapeutic Infrastructure: Every community needs access to trauma-informed counseling, elder circles, youth listening tables, and emotional literacy programs. If we don't treat the wounds, we'll infect the wealth.

And most of all — spiritual discipline. Not religion. Not control. But the understanding that your ego is not God. That legacy is communal. That when you lead, you do it as a servant, not a celebrity.

Closing Note:

We always talk about rebuilding what we lost. But the truth is: some of us were never taught how to lead what we gain.

Power without healing is just tyranny in new clothes.

Land is nothing without stewardship. Funds are nothing without trust. A village is nothing without vision that lasts longer than one man's ego.

We can build it. But the question remains…

Can we keep it?

CHAPTER 32

Wealth That Feeds Itself: Community Capital, Not Just Cash

STORY: "The $5 Dream and the $50 Billion Truth"

Malik stood in line at the gas station with a $5 bill in his hand. Behind him, a kid was begging his mom for snacks, and an older man was talking to the cashier about hitting a lick on a scratch-off ticket. Malik wasn't broke, but he wasn't free either. He worked, paid bills, and tried to save — but something always came up. He looked at the lottery machines and thought, Even if I hit, it wouldn't change nothing for real. I'd still be alone with the money.

That night, he sat in his apartment watching a YouTube video about Jewish credit unions and how they fund each other's dreams, homes, and businesses with collective capital. No begging banks. No GoFundMes. Just trust and accountability.

Malik paused the video and whispered to himself, "That's the difference. They got community capital. We just got cash."

PSYCHOLOGICAL BREAKDOWN

The Black community has been taught to chase income, not infrastructure. We flex paychecks but lack pooled power. We build individual wealth that dies with the person, not group systems that feed generations.

Wealth that feeds itself requires trust — something colonization, slavery, and economic sabotage stripped from our DNA. They didn't just steal labor; they destroyed the instinct to move as one. Now we have "I got mine" syndrome. We stunt for the 'Gram but never organize like immigrants who rotate funds through susu systems, LLC webs, and land trusts.

We fear scams more than we fear staying broke. That's trauma.

CORPORATE POV VS STREET POV

Corporate: Corporations don't just make money. They protect and grow it through layered entities, capital reinvestment, private equity circles, and tax loopholes. They don't spend — they cycle.

Street: On the block, it's fast money and faster spending. One win equals one flex. Nobody reinvests in the trap. There's no group re-up fund. No exit plan. Just survival spending and social pressure to look rich.

The corporations build empires. The streets build debt.

CENTRAL CONCERN

Concern: How can we build wealth that feeds itself if we don't trust each other enough to pool and protect capital?

The distrust is real. Scams. Abandonment. Past failures. Everyone got a cousin who stole, a group that folded, or an elder who mismanaged funds. The trauma is generational.

But the alternative is worse. The absence of group capital means we keep going to banks that redline us, landlords who hate us, and jobs that drain us. Our wealth ends at funeral homes and courtrooms — never in trusts, Roth IRAs, or business equity.

STRATEGIC SOLUTION

We must move from cash flow to capital architecture. That means:

Internal Credit Unions: Community-owned financial hubs that give loans to members with trackable oversight. No outside interest.

Rotating Investment Circles: Trusted small pods that vote and rotate capital with contracts and consequences — not just vibes.

Community Roth IRAs & Retirement Pools: If 1,000 members contributed $20/week into a Roth structure, you'd hit millions in tax-free capital within 10 years — all protected from probate.

Emergency & Venture Funds: Pooling $1/month per member creates emergency access without banks. Adding $10/month per member builds seed capital for community-owned businesses.

Micro-banking Teams: Trained members assigned to track funds, hold receipts, enforce rules. Just like private banks — but accountable to us.

This is not a dream. This is math and discipline.

CLOSING TRUTH

It ain't easy. Most people won't trust a dollar unless it's in their hand. But what good is your dollar if it dies with you?

You trusted white banks for 40 years and still got denied a home loan. What do you really have to lose?

The real risk is staying broke because we feared each other more than we feared poverty.

One man with a million dollars can build nothing without help.
A thousand men with $100 each can build a new world.

QUOTE FROM THE REMEMBERER:

"The wealth you keep alone feeds only the worms.
The wealth you build together feeds the unborn."

Chapter 33: When Black Dreams Get Rezoned

Story: The Field That Was Ours

There was a small neighborhood in East Atlanta that used to be all Black. Brick duplexes, corner stores with faded signs, and a barbershop that doubled as a city council complaint line. At the center of the block was a wide, open lot. Kids played football there, elders gathered there, and food vendors sold ribs and watermelon slices under tents every summer.

One day, white city planners showed up taking pictures. Nobody thought much of it. A few weeks later, trucks rolled in, and "Public Notice" signs went up — rezoning was on the table. The neighbors didn't understand the paperwork. They didn't show up to the hearings. Within 18 months, the land was marked "mixed-use." New condos replaced the lot. The barbershop was bought and repainted gray. That field — once ours — was now home to a dog park with artificial turf and Wi-Fi.

A family on that block had lived there for 44 years. Paid their mortgage off early. But when the property taxes tripled, they couldn't afford it. The land was never lost in a war. It was stolen through rezoning, silence, and paperwork.

Psychological Breakdown: The Invisible Eviction

The modern eviction of Black communities doesn't always happen with sheriffs and locks. It happens with zoning maps, tax hikes, development grants, and the illusion of "progress." This is warfare dressed in bureaucracy. It's easier to steal land from people who don't know how land works.

Many Black communities aren't trained in the language of zoning, permitting, easements, or land trust protections. This ignorance becomes generational eviction. Land gets sold "for cheap" because taxes are high, paperwork is overwhelming, or families don't know the value of what they own. The field doesn't get bulldozed — it gets quietly repurposed by design.

Corporate POV vs Street POV

Corporate POV:
"Rezoning is about growth, expansion, and maximizing the value of underutilized land."
Translation: We see your community as profit margins and opportunity zones.

Street POV:
"They taking everything — block by block. And we ain't even know we was supposed to fight back."
Translation: We see the loss but not the process. We know something's wrong, but we can't name the moves.

The street fights with passion. The corporation fights with paperwork. The system always bets that we won't read the fine print.

Central Concern: Why We Lose What We Don't Understand

The biggest threat to Black communities isn't always violence — it's unfamiliarity with the systems shaping the land beneath our feet. When you don't understand zoning laws, property tax liens, redevelopment incentives, or eminent domain, you end up surrendering your home with a signature instead of a fight.

This lack of education has turned property owners into lifelong renters in disguise. It's the reason so many family homes are lost after a grandmother dies — nobody knew to file probate or set up a trust. We call it "gentrification," but the real weapon is legal ignorance and the speed of strategic paperwork.

Strategic Solution: Legal Literacy + Land Lockdown

1. Zoning Education Hubs
Every Black community needs a local council or nonprofit teaching zoning, land use policy, tax mitigation, and deed protection. Teach people how to read the maps and know when rezoning is happening before it passes.

2. Lock the Land in Trusts or Co-ops
Land should not be owned individually unless the family has legal succession planning in place. Create community land trusts or co-ops that hold land as a group, with bylaws that prevent predatory buyouts.

3. Tax Armor Through LLCs & Nonprofits
Homes and lots should be owned by family LLCs or nonprofit entities where appropriate. This helps reduce liability, keeps control within the family, and allows access to grant programs or legal protections.

4. Fight with Paper, Not Protest Alone
Send people to city zoning meetings. File objections. Draft petitions. Submit alternate development proposals. Once we learn their language, we can't be silenced.

5. Teach Heirs Property Law Early
Most Black-owned land lost in the South is due to "heirs property" — land passed down without a will. This must be

fixed now through legal aid programs and community estate planning drives.

Final Words: The Field Still Lives in Us

We must understand that the field — that open lot, that house your grandfather built, that church on the corner — is not just a location. It is legacy. And when you lose land, you don't just lose dirt. You lose leverage. You lose lineage. You lose a place to anchor your children's dreams.

They rezoned us because they knew we didn't know what zoning was.
They priced us out because they knew we didn't know how to contest the price.
They took the land while we were busy surviving.

But the next war is different. The new soldier reads contracts. The new soldier files deeds. The new soldier attends city council meetings in work boots and a tailored suit.

We're no longer just fighting for land. We're fighting for memory.

Chapter 34 — Blueprints, Not Blue Checks: How Status Got Swapped for Substance

The Parable: “The Architect and the Influencer”

In a city half-rebuilt from riots, two men stood on opposite ends of the same street. One had blueprints in his hands. The other had blue checks on his screen.

The Architect was never flashy. He wore work boots and had graphite smudged fingers. He’d spent years designing a block—each building planned for Black families, businesses, a health clinic, even a school. No news cameras came. No applause. Just sweat and blueprints.

The Influencer, across the street, was dripped out. Designer sneakers, chains, perfectly lit selfies. His followers ran deep—millions watched his motivational videos, laughed at his skits, commented “King” under every post. He spoke of Black excellence but owned no property, employed no people, and built no systems.

One day, a developer came to the block with an offer: “I’ll buy this land. One of you can choose what we build here. Who got the community behind them?”

The crowd swarmed the Influencer, hypnotized by his fame.

The land was sold. Condos rose where clinics were meant to go. Rent soared. Displacement followed.

The Architect folded his blueprints and walked away silent. The city never realized what they’d lost until it was too late.

The Concern: Status Has Been Rebranded, and It's Costing Us Everything

We live in a time where perceived power is more popular than actual power.

Our people—especially the youth—have been socially engineered to chase visibility over viability. We trade land for likes. We swap tangible legacy for algorithm clout. We let the image of success replace the function of success.

What used to be a symbol of freedom—owning something, feeding your family, teaching the next generation—has been overshadowed by carefully curated aesthetics: foreign whips with no insurance, borrowed jewelry, digital fame with no infrastructure behind it.

The danger? A whole generation believes they're "winning" because they're seen, not because they're sovereign.

Psychological Breakdown: The Performance Trap and the Scarcity Theater

This isn't just cultural—this is psychological warfare.

When you come from nothing, the performance of having something can feel like power. You post your steak dinner because you remember when ramen was your only option. You show the designer belt because you were ashamed of hand-me-downs.

The system profits off this trauma-response.

Social media weaponizes dopamine. It rewards exaggeration, not elevation. It turns our pain into platforms and trains us to commodify our struggle instead of solving it. We're caught in scarcity theater—everyone trying to look rich in an economy that makes us poorer by the year.

True wealth is silent. Power moves in shadows. Ownership doesn't scream.

Corporate POV vs. Street POV

Corporate Side:
The Fortune 500 companies don't flaunt—they accumulate. Warren Buffett still lives in the same house. Amazon warehouses don't have neon signs, but they control global logistics. They build under radar, acquire without alerting, and stay private until power is locked in.

Street Side:
Meanwhile, the hustler with a $100K car and $300K in jewelry might not own the house his mom lives in. He's visible but vulnerable. And the system loves visible targets—it's easier to tax, to audit, to trap. The more we show, the less we grow.

Lesson: You Don't Need Attention—You Need Leverage

The game was never about being seen. It's about being positioned.

Land gives you leverage.

Businesses give you leverage.

Skill sets give you leverage.

Silence gives you leverage.

Control of the supply chain gives you leverage.

Everything else is noise.

Until we teach our people the power of blueprints—long-term planning, quiet building, patience over performance—we will keep losing neighborhoods to people who never flash but always own.

Case Studies:

Black Panther Party vs. Modern Celebrity Activism:
The Panthers had no platforms, no social media, but they built food programs, clinics, and educational hubs. They got watched by the FBI not because they were loud, but because they were effective.

Killer Mike's Barbershop Model:
He doesn't just rap about empowerment—he owns the buildings. Real estate in Atlanta. He employs barbers, builds economic loops. Quiet moves, loud impact.

Jay-Z's 4:44 vs. Rap Culture:
One album where he rapped about generational wealth, buying art, credit, and Black legacy—but much of the culture still glorifies debt, chains, and fast flexes. It shows how hard it is to shift collective mindset when flash wins the algorithm.

The Solution: Status Must Be Re-Defined in Our Communities

We have to reprogram the definition of winning. Make land sexy. Make clinics legendary. Make skill trades noble. Make financial literacy viral.

Put the pressure on strategy, not on selfies.

Elevate people who employ, not just entertain.

Praise the father who fixes his credit.

Celebrate the woman who owns her home before 30.

Respect the young brother building a farm instead of followers.

We must stop clapping for actors playing rich and start funding architects building freedom.

Closing Reminder: It's Not Easy—But It's Necessary

It's tempting to chase the spotlight. It's addictive to feel seen. But we can't build sovereignty on validation. We can only build it on discipline, vision, and sacrifice.

No one claps for the foundation.

But the foundation is what keeps the house from falling.

And we don't need more mansions in collapse. We need more cornerstones that last.

From the Blueprint of Patrice Shabazz

When they tell you you need a brand, say: I'm building a bank.
When they say go viral, say: I went legal.

When they ask why you're so quiet, say: Because I'm owning things too powerful to speak on.

You don't need a blue check.
You need a blueprint.

That's what they fear most.

The Sovereign Blueprint: 1,000 Acres of Freedom

By Patrice Shabazz

PART I – THE CHARTER (Constitution & Bylaws)

Article I – Land and Purpose

1. This community shall secure and steward **1,000 acres of land**, divided and managed for the survival, growth, and sovereignty of its 1,000 members.
2. The purpose is to create a **self-sustaining, Black-owned, sovereign village** that cannot be bought, broken, or erased by outside forces.
3. All members agree that **individual gain never outweighs collective survival**.

Article II – Land Division (1,000 Acres)

- **Residential Housing: 400 acres**
  - Triple-wides, double-wides, single-wides, mobile homes, RV lots, built homes, and 2 quadplexes.
  - **Target: 300 family units + 200 single units + 100 RV studios = 1,000 residents comfortably.**

    - Average unit density: 1 home per acre, with shared utilities.
- **Agriculture & Livestock: 250 acres**
    - Crop farming (120 acres): corn, beans, collards, sweet potatoes, herbs.
    - Livestock (80 acres): goats, chickens, cows, ducks, geese, rabbits, sheep, turkeys, pigs.
    - Aquaponics & greenhouses (20 acres).
    - Orchards/vineyards (20 acres).
    - Apiary & pollination zones (10 acres).
- **Business & Trades: 100 acres**
    - Mechanic shop (3 acres).
    - Construction & lumber yard (10 acres).
    - Electric/solar hub (5 acres).
    - Plumbing/sanitation center (5 acres).
    - Community market/grocery store (7 acres).
    - Barber, beauty, tailoring, shoe repair (5 acres).
    - Content/media studio (5 acres).
    - Tech/web hub (3 acres).
    - Credit union & treasury (3 acres).
    - Legal & print shop (2 acres).
    - Event/venue rental space (10 acres).
    - Recycling/compost & tool library (7 acres).
    - Childcare/Montessori center (10 acres).
    - Retreat/wellness spa (5 acres).
    - Total reserved for growth: 20 acres.
- **Education & Healthcare: 80 acres**
    - K-12 School & Vocational Training Center (40 acres).
    - Clinic & Holistic Healing Center (20 acres).
    - Cultural Memory School (10 acres).
    - Expansion for university-level trades (10 acres).
- **Recreation & Communal: 60 acres**
    - Sports courts, outdoor gym, walking trails.

- Gathering amphitheater for rites, rituals, events.
    - Parks & meditation gardens.
- **Burial Grounds: 40 acres**
    - Divided into sacred sections: elders, children, warriors, community founders.
    - Maintained by "Keepers of Memory."
- **Utilities & Infrastructure: 70 acres**
    - Solar farms, wells, water storage.
    - Septic & waste management.
    - Cell towers/internet hub.
    - Emergency storage (food, fuel, medical).
- **Wild Reserve & Expansion Buffer: 100 acres**
    - Hunting, fishing, timber.
    - Reserved for future homes, factories, or luxury additions.

Article III – Housing Structure

1. Housing types:
    - **Triple-wides (40 units)** – Large families & elders.
    - **Double-wides (80 units)** – Mid-size families.
    - **Single-wides (80 units)** – Couples/singles.
    - **Mobile homes (100 units)** – Flexible living.
    - **RV studios (100 units)** – Singles, re-entry, or transitional.
    - **Built homes (40)** – Long-term leaders & families of honor.
    - **Quadplexes (2 buildings = 8 units)** – Transitional or visiting guests.
2. Housing remains **community-owned**, leased to members under agreements.

3. Eviction/removal requires review by Elders + People's Assembly vote.

Article IV – Governance

1. **Council of Elders (7 members)** – Spiritual & cultural leadership. Final authority on rituals, moral law, excommunication, and sacred matters.
2. **Operational Committee (10 members)** – Oversee farming, trades, housing, education, health, and utilities.
3. **Financial Board (5 members)** – Handle treasury, Roth IRAs, pensions, savings, credit union, and audits.
4. **People's Assembly (all adults 18+)** – Monthly/quarterly votes on policy, leadership reviews, and amendments.
5. **Emergency Override Protocol** – Activated only in disaster, with temporary chain of command.

Article V – Economic Structure

1. **Credit Union** – Holds all funds, operates low-interest loans, leases vehicles, manages Roth IRA contributions.
2. **Internal Businesses** – Each trade (mechanic, farm, clinic, school) is a community-owned enterprise. Profits circulate back.
3. **Revenue Streams**:
    - Food production + market sales.
    - Media + content creation.
    - Vocational school tuition (outside students).

   - Construction/electric contracts outside community.
   - Retreat + event rentals.
   - Long-term: luxury fleet leasing, branded products.
4. **Member Contribution** – 35–40 hours/week labor or trade.

Article VI – Legal Structure

1. Registered as **multi-entity hybrid**:
   - **Land Trust** for land ownership.
   - **Nonprofit arm** for schools/clinic (grants).
   - **LLC or Cooperative Corp** for businesses.
   - **501(d)** as communal treasury.
2. **Legal Defense Infrastructure**:
   - Rotating legal fund.
   - 3-lawyer partnerships.
   - In-house paralegals.
   - Monthly legal literacy clinics.

Article VII – Family & Justice

1. **Community Family Court** – Handles custody, marriage, inheritance.
2. **Code of Conduct** – Zero tolerance for theft, assault, sabotage.
3. **Conflict Resolution Circle** – Mandatory before external court.
4. **Marriage Agreements** – Prenup-style contracts.
5. **Custody Agreements** – Set before children are born.

6. **Death & Burial Protocol** – Wills required; funeral handled in-house.

Article VIII – Security

1. **Community Safety Corps** – Trained, armed, and legal defense unit.
2. Patrols only community land.
3. Must remain defensive, never offensive.
4. Required monthly training in: firearms, first aid, survival.

Article IX – Rituals & Identity

1. **Monthly Ritual Calendar** – Replaces Western holidays with ancestral ceremonies.
2. **Rites of Passage** – Flame Walk, Voice Ceremony, Name Year.
3. **Symbols** – Tri-Spire Flame, Seed & Spear, Open Eye.
4. **Oath of Entry**:
   "I do not come to live only for myself. I come to remember, protect, and build. My hands are clean. My heart is willing. I am one with this fire."

Article X – Finances & Member Benefits

1. Every member receives:
   - Housing, food, healthcare access.
   - Roth IRA & group retirement support.

    - Legal aid.
    - Transportation fleet access.
    - Education & training.
2. Every member contributes:
    - 35–40 hrs/week labor.
    - Respect for rituals.
    - Participation in voting & security drills.

PART II – THE PROPHETIC MANUAL

Chapter 1: Why 1,000 Acres?

Because 100 acres ain't enough. 300 acres won't feed us. 500 acres will only get swallowed by time. But 1,000 acres—that's sovereignty. That's a square mile and a half of **Black-owned soil**. Enough for housing, schools, burial grounds, businesses, food, and future generations. Enough to say, **we don't rent—we rule.**

Chapter 2: The Math of Survival

- **Land Cost** – Rural NC, SC, GA, TN land averages $5k–$10k per acre.
    - **1,000 acres = $5M–$10M.**
    - With negotiation & distressed sales, target **$3.5M–$4.5M.**
- **Housing**:
    - RV conversions: $5k–$15k each.
    - Single-wides: $35k–$50k.
    - Double-wides: $60k–$90k.

- Triple-wides: $120k–$150k.
- Built homes: $200k each.

Housing as Dignity, Not Division

In this community, housing is not about status. It's about function, discipline, and contribution. Everyone pays the same $12,000 buy-in, and everyone lives with dignity. The difference in housing types is based on what the community needs — not who has the biggest pockets. Every unit, from the RV camp to the built homes, will be kept clean, landscaped, and maintained daily so that no one feels "less than." Our people will walk outside proud, whether they're in a triple-wide or a quadplex, because the entire village looks good.

The RV Community: The Flagship of Unity

The RV camp will be more than housing — it will be the heartbeat of the village. Located closest to the main amenities, it will offer:

Concrete walkways and rose bushes at every lot

Power hookups, fenced yards, and storage sheds

A shared bar lounge with multiple TVs, smoke area, pool table, and couches — the community's social hub

Laundry and tailoring access so everyone looks sharp daily

Leadership Example: Even I, the founder, will live here — not in the built homes, but in the RV camp. This proves the vision is about unity, not hierarchy. Nobody can say others are "better off" when the leader himself is living shoulder-to-shoulder with the people.

Triple-Wides & Double-Wides: The Family Anchors

These homes will house large and mid-sized families. They'll be placed near schools, playgrounds, and health clinics for easy access. Features include:

Spacious yards with room for gardens

Housekeeping and landscaping crews to keep every unit clean

Family support resources like parenting workshops, childcare centers, and tutoring programs

Emergency maintenance teams on-call to fix water, power, or safety issues within hours

These are the backbone of the village — where families raise children and build stability for generations.

Single-Wides & Mobile Homes: The Builders' Row

For couples, small families, or individuals, these homes offer flexibility and affordability without losing dignity. Each will come with:

Front porches and landscaped lots so they still look like homes, not boxes

Access to community trades (plumbing, HVAC, carpentry) for upgrades or customization

Clothing and grooming co-ops nearby to ensure no one looks run down

Rotating maintenance patrols to keep every home crisp and functional

This section will likely house many of the hustlers, tradespeople, and teachers — the ones building the day-to-day systems of the community.

Built Homes: Honor & Legacy

Only 40 of these permanent structures will exist — designed for elders, long-term leaders, healers, and families of honor. But even here, dignity is equal. These homes won't look like mansions towering over others. They'll look like anchors. Features:

Durable construction (brick, modular, or earthbag) built to last for generations

Cultural landscaping with gardens, trees, and spaces for meditation

Resource hubs inside — some homes may double as meeting spots, clinics, or study centers

Legacy assignments — when an elder passes, the home is reassigned to another pillar family, not flipped or sold

These homes will symbolize the village's roots, but they won't separate people. They'll blend into the overall flow so nobody feels "less than."

Quadplexes: Transition & Support Housing

With only 2 quadplexes (8 units total), these spaces are for transitional housing — young couples, single parents, or visiting relatives. They will be:

Centrally located for quick access to schools, health care, and the RV lounge

Maintained weekly with cleaning services

Furnished with essentials so people can get stable fast

Connected to mentorship programs so every transition leads to long-term stability

Resources & Services Shared Across All Housing

No matter where you live, you will have access to:

Housekeeping & Landscaping Crews → daily rotation, no slums, no neglect

Laundry Services & Clothing Co-op → every resident has clean, professional-quality clothes

Barber/Beauty Care → dignity in grooming for men, women, and children

Maintenance Patrols → in-house plumbers, electricians, HVAC, carpenters on call 24/7

Food Access → meal service for elders, community kitchen options, grocery store co-op

Community Wardrobe → tailoring, shoe repair, and seasonal clothing so no one looks ragged

Wellness Support → access to the clinic, counseling, and holistic healers within walking distance

The Standard of Dignity

This is not an "American trailer park." This is a sovereign village. Nobody here will walk around in rags. Nobody will live in a broken-down unit. Nobody will feel inferior. Our people will look sharp, live clean, and carry themselves with dignity, because ownership makes even the smallest unit powerful.

When you walk up to your home — whether it's a built house or an RV — you'll see:

Landscaped roses and walkways

A front porch you can be proud of

Neighbors whose homes are just as clean and sharp as yours

This isn't about housing tiers. This is about a standard of life we all agree to uphold.

- **Initial Infrastructure** (first 5 years):
    - Wells + septic: $500k.
    - Solar: $1M.
    - Roads & utilities: $1.5M.
    - Clinic & school: $2M.
    - Fleet vehicles: $2M.
    - Farms/livestock startup: $500k.

Total Startup: $8M–$10M.
Not a dream—**a number.**

Chapter 3: The Burial Ground Promise

Too many of us die and get shipped to white-owned cemeteries. Our bones rest in land we don't own. Here, **40 acres are sacred**—one acre for every 25 people. Elders in one section, children in another, warriors and founders set apart. Every funeral becomes an oath: *"We bury you in soil that is ours."*

Chapter 4: Work as Freedom

Forget jobs that drain you. Here, work **feeds your children, builds your house, grows your food, cuts your hair, repairs your car, and defends your land.** Thirty-five hours a week for your own. That's not slavery—that's liberation disguised as labor.

Chapter 5: The Money Trap Ends Here

Instead of begging banks, we become our own bank.

- Community Credit Union.
- Fleet leasing under our LLC.
- Roth IRAs managed collectively.
- Internal pension fund.
  No predatory loans. No redlining. No foreclosure scams. **Only circulation.**

Chapter 6: The Security Truth

Call it what it is—a militia—but call it wisely. To the public: "Community Safety Corps." To the people: a shield. Trained in law, medicine, arms, and defense. Never offensive, always ready. **We will never be caught defenseless again.**

Chapter 7: Rituals Replace Holidays

No more Christmas debt. No more 4th of July lies. Instead:

- **Rebirth in March** (our new year).
- **Shadow Night in January** (confession & cleansing).
- **Firewalk in June** (rites of passage).
- **Memory Month in October** (ancestors & lessons).

This is how culture survives—not Hallmark cards.

Chapter 8: Generational Wealth, Not Generational Rent

Every child grows up with **land, trade skills, education, Roth IRA, and protection.** They inherit not just a will, but a world.

Chapter 9: Expansion Beyond 1,000

The buffer land is our insurance. After we stabilize 1,000 acres, we expand to 2,000, then 5,000. Every success funds the next. This is not a one-off—it's a **nation within a nation.**

Final Manifesto

This land is not a fantasy. It is a plan. It is not utopia. It is **work, sweat, blood, law, and unity.** But if we do it, our children will never beg another system for survival again.

1,000 acres. 1,000 people. 1,000 futures.

Closing Manifesto: The Resurrection of Us

We are not poor. We are programmed.
We are not lazy. We are misled.
We are not broken. We are fragmented—scattered across the map, chasing approval from systems that were never designed to elevate us.

This book was never just about economics. It was about reactivating memory.
The memory of a people who once controlled trade routes, who built thriving towns from red clay and vision. Who healed themselves with herbs and held councils under moonlight. Who grew crops on their land, and when that land was stolen, built again from scratch. And again. And again.

Until they forgot.

The great trick of colonization wasn't just slavery. It was the psychological erasure of self-sufficiency. They replaced our drums with clocks. Our villages with job titles. Our generational wealth with monthly paychecks. Our bartering systems with debt-based plastic cards. Our community tables with fast food chains.

And once they fractured our unity, they sold us individualism like freedom.

But now the spell is breaking.

This book is not written in theory—it is etched from truth. From soil-testing land to fiber-optic infrastructure, from raising goats to raising governance standards. From mobile home parks with economic rotation to security councils who vote on discipline, not just punishment. From buying used fleet trucks in bulk to buying back the minds of men who forgot they were kings.

We do not need 40 acres and a mule. We need 500 acres and a blueprint.

We've already proven we can build wealth. Black Wall Street wasn't a fluke. It was a formula. But desegregation made us fall in love with white validation and forget that we were once the storeowners, the teachers, the architects, the doctors, the protectors.

Now we want promotions from people who don't know our names. We want inclusion in a house that was built on our backs but not for our benefit. We keep applying for chairs at tables where our grandfathers once carved the wood.

We must stop.

This book declares the end of begging.
This book is a funeral for dependency.
This book is a resurrection.

We no longer have the excuse of ignorance. It has been replaced with instruction. You now know the layout. You know the soil. You know the housing, the animal breeds, the vehicle strategy, the trade rotations, the schooling design, the legal defense, the economic cycle.

You know.

Now the only question is: will you build?

This is the final time we ask.

The world doesn't owe us unity. We owe it to ourselves.
Because we are the land.
We are the labor.
We are the architects.
We are the product.
We are the protectors.
We are the law.
We are the bank.
We are the dream.
We are the answer.

And as of today—we are no longer for sale.

The era of renting respect is over. Ownership begins now.
Welcome to the new blueprint.
Welcome to Group Economics.
Welcome back to us.

About the Author

Patrice Shabazz is a son of North Carolina — raised by hardship, hardened by experience, and healed through truth. A sharp voice forged in poverty, he writes to expose the systems that keep everyday people buried under debt, silence, and struggle. His words don't just teach — they testify.

Patrice's mission reaches beyond the page. He is actively working to build a self-sustainable community rooted in group economics, accountability, and liberation. Through books, outreach, and strategic action, he's not just telling stories — he's blueprinting solutions.

If you are a like-minded individual, a builder, a visionary, or simply someone curious about how we rise together, reach out: patriceshabazz39@gmail.com

—

"A lone runner may reach the hill first — but a village crosses mountains."
— Patrice Shabazz

Led by Patrice Shabazz | Founder, Exclusive Heights

We're building more than a neighborhood — we're building a future.

The Vision

Imagine 300–500 acres of land, powered by solar, growing our own food, raising livestock, creating jobs, and raising children in a safe, educated, self-governed environment.

This isn't a dream. This is a blueprint.

We're forming a 1,000-person self-sustainable Black-led community rooted in:

- Group economics
- Cooperative living
- Clean food, clean water, clean energy
- Vocational training & land-based education
- Mental, physical, and financial healing

—

The Math & Mission

- Goal: $12,000 per person x 1,000 = $12 million
- Covers: Land (300–500 acres), infrastructure, housing, farming, solar, schools, tradespaces, and startup capital for community-owned businesses.

Every dollar goes into ownership, food security, and generational wealth — not rent.

—

Who We're Looking For

We're recruiting:

- Skilled tradespeople: Electricians, Plumbers, Builders, Farmers, HVAC, Welders
- Educators & Mentors: Teachers, Counselors, Homeschoolers, Youth Leaders
- Medical & Holistic Health: Nurses, CNAs, Herbalists, Wellness Coaches
- Tech & Media: Web Designers, Editors, Content Creators
- General Builders: Visionaries willing to work, grow, and invest in change

—

Why Join?

- Be part of a legacy project
- Live and work with purpose
- Help build Black independence
- Escape survival mode and enter sustainability
- Your name will be on the foundation of a new nation within a nation

—

Support & Donate

Help fund the first phase:

- [GoFundMe gofund.me/637427e2]
- Cash App: $ExclusiveHeights

Every donation brings us one step closer to land, infrastructure, and freedom.

—

Get Involved

Contact: patriceshabazz39@gmail.com
Based in North Carolina — open to national collaboration

—

"A system built to bury us… won't survive the ones who plant back."

— Patrice Shabazz